INTRODUCTION

Welcome to the *Precepts For Living® Personal Study Guide!* When using it, we hope that you will find it to be an enlightening and rewarding experience. This study guide can be used as a reference tool for any teacher or student who is serious about learning and knowing the inspired Word of God. It is designed to be used in conjunction with the *Precepts For Living® Annual Commentary.* It should help you get the God-intended meaning of each Scripture presented and explained in *Precepts.* Therefore, it is suggested that you use the guide in the following way:

• First, thoroughly study each lesson of *Precepts.*

• Then go to the companion lesson in this study guide and answer all the questions pertaining to the lesson.

• After you have answered all the questions for a particular lesson *on your own,* check your answers by using the **Answer Key,** which is found in the back of the book.

• If you miss an answer, go back and research it in *Precepts.* This will enhance both your learning experience and memorization of Scripture.

Enjoy this *Precepts For Living® Personal Study Guide.* As you do your Bible study, observe Scripture, grasp it by correctly interpreting the text, and then walk in the knowledge of God's Word.

TABLE OF CONTENTS

PRECEPTS FOR LIVING® PERSONAL STUDY GUIDE

UMI MISSION STATEMENT: *We are called of God to create, produce, and distribute quality Christian education products; to deliver exemplary customer service; and to provide quality Christian educational services, which will empower God's people, especially within the Black community, to evangelize, disciple, and equip people for serving Christ, His kingdom, and church.*

Precepts For Living® Personal Study Guide, Vol. 4, No. 1, September 2009–August 2010. Published yearly by UMI (Urban Ministries, Inc.), P. O. Box 436987, Chicago, IL 60643-6987. Founder and Chairman: Melvin E. Banks Sr., Litt.D.; President and CEO: C. Jeffrey Wright, J.D.; Vice President of Editorial: Cheryl Price, Ph.D.; Directors of Editorial: Ed Gilbreath, Rosa Sailes, Ed.D.; Editorial Writer: Evangeline Carey; Cover Designer: Trinidad Zavala; Interior Designer: Bruce Donaldson. Lessons based on International Sunday School Lessons; the International Bible Lessons for Christian Teaching. Copyright© 2005 by the Committee on the Uniform Series. Used by permission. Supplementary Lesson Development. Copyright© 2008 by UMI. All rights reserved. $7.95 per copy (postage included). Printed in the U.S.A. **NO PART OF THIS PUBLICATION MAY BE REPRODUCED IN ANY FORM WITHOUT THE WRITTEN PERMISSION OF THE PUBLISHER. To Order:** Contact your local Christian bookstore; call UMI at **1-800-860-8642**; or visit our website at **www.urbanministries.com**.

TABLE OF CONTENTS

PRECEPTS FOR LIVING® PERSONAL STUDY GUIDE

"Have not I commanded thee? Be strong and of good courage; be not afraid, neither be thou dismayed: for the Lord thy God is with thee whithersoever thou goest" (Joshua 1:9).

JOSHUA: A LEADER FOR THE PEOPLE

JOSHUA 1:1–11; 16–17

Use with Bible Study Guide 1.

WORDS AND PHRASES

Match the words, phrases, or names with the correct definitions.

1. ____ commission
2. ____ courage
3. ____ Joshua

4. ____ meditate
5. ____ minister
6. ____ officer

7. ____ prosperity
8. ____ Schechem
9. ____ strong
10. ___ the Promised Land

a. someone who waits on or attends as a servant to another
b. Canaan—the place promised to Abraham and his descendents
c. where Abraham erected an altar that symbolizes the Covenant Promise between God and him
d. being steadfast or brave; behaving valiantly
e. progress in everything one does; being successful
f. sufficiently alert, physically or mentally, to face danger, fear or difficulty
g. Moses' successor as the human leader for the people
h. to mutter, murmur, ponder, study, and speak
i. overseer, superintendent, and magistrate
j. a charge, appointment, authorization

JUMP-STARTING THE LESSON

11. According to the In Focus story, Joshua has to walk in Moses' shoes as he leads the people to the Promised Land.　　　True　　　False

12. According to the In Focus story, Joshua must lead as _____ _____ him to lead.

UNDERSTANDING THE LESSON

13. Following God's instructions, Abraham, his wife _____, and nephew _____, leave Abraham's birthplace of _____ of the _____ (see The People, Places, and Times).

14. Joshua's birth name was "_____", which means "_____" (see Background).

15. For _____ years, Moses leads the _____ and oftentimes _____ Children of Israel in the _____ (see Background).

16. "Joshua" means "_____ _____" (Joshua 1:1–2, In Depth).

17. The book of Joshua is a continuation of the narrative in the Book of _____ (see Introduction, MLOT).

18. The land that God is giving Israel extends from the _____ in the _____ boundary to _____ in the North, and from the river Euphrates (in the present-day _____) in the East to the great _____ Sea (Joshua 1:3–4, MLOT).

COMMITTING TO THE WORD

19. According to Joshua 1:6, God told Joshua to "Be strong and of a good courage: for unto this people shalt thou divide for an inheritance the land, which I sware unto their fathers to give them." Explain what this passage means.

_____

_____

_____

_____

_____

WALKING IN THE WORD

20. Explain what God meant when He said, according to Joshua 1:8, "This book of the law shall not depart out of thy mouth; but thou shalt meditate therein day and night, that thou mayest observe to do according to all that is written therein." Then explain how this Scripture applies to your own life.

_____

_____

_____

_____

_____

_____

_____

_____

"And the LORD looked upon him, and said, Go in this thy might, and thou shalt save Israel from the hand of the Midianites: have not I sent thee?"
(Judges 6:14).

GIDEON: A DELIVERER FOR THE PEOPLE

JUDGES 6:1–3, 7–14

Use with Bible Study Guide 2.

WORDS AND PHRASES

Match the words, phrases, or names with the correct definitions.

1. ____ adversaries
2. ____ Baal and the Asheroth
3. ____ compromise
4. ____ "In this thy might"
5. ____ "Midian"
6. ____ "mighty man of valour"
7. ____ Ophrah
8. ____ prevail
9. ____ the Midianites
10. ____ thresh

a. to be stout, strengthen, to be strong
b. great or powerful warrior; a strong and valiant man
c. territory allotted to the tribe of Manasseh
d. to beat out in order to separate
e. enemies
f. pagan gods that Israel worshiped
g. the enemies and persecutors of Israel
h. concession, conciliation
i. means "strife"
j. human strength or power

JUMP-STARTING THE LESSON

11. According to the In Focus story, why is it that God often cuts away a man's self-confidence?

_____

_____

_____

12. According to the In Focus story, Gideon's adequacy will come from _____.

UNDERSTANDING THE LESSON

13. Approximately how many years does the period of the Judges cover (see The People, Places, and Times)?
a. 100   b. 200   c. 300   d. 400

14. The office of judge was hereditary (see The People, Places, and Times). True   False

15. A cycle of _____ and _____, _____, and lapse back into _____ is repeated throughout Judges (see Background).

16. Paraphrase the question that Gideon asked the angel of the Lord, who brought him the message that God had chosen him to lead the people (Judges 6:13, In Depth, More Light on the Text). Then tell what it means.

_____

_____

_____

_____

17. Why was Gideon secretly threshing wheat by the winepress when the angel found him? (Judges 6:11, In Depth, More Light on the Text).

_____

_____

_____

_____

18. Gideon felt that the Lord had abandoned Israel and turned them over to their enemies (Judges 6:12–13, More Light on the Text).   True   False

COMMITTING TO THE WORD
Fill in the blanks.
19. God's strength is _____ in our _____ (Judges 6:14, More Light on the Text).

WALKING IN THE WORD
20. What does the statement "The Lord is with you" mean in your own life?

_____

_____

_____

_____

_____

_____

_____

> *"And said, O my God, I am ashamed and blush to lift up my face to thee, my God: for our iniquities are increased over our head, and our trespass is grown up unto the heavens" (Ezra 9:6).*

EZRA: A PRIEST FOR THE PEOPLE

EZRA 9:5–11, 15

Use with Bible Study Guide 3.

WORDS AND PHRASES

Match the words, phrases, or names with the correct definitions.

1. ____ abomination
2. ____ a Scribe
3. ____ desolation
4. ____ Ezra
5. ____ heaviness
6. ____ iniquities
7. ____ righteous
8. ____ Shaphan
9. ____ trespass
10. ___ unclean

a. He read the Book of the Law to King Josiah.
b. morally impure
c. something that is morally disgusting
d. mischief, fault, or sin
e. copyist of the Hebrew Scriptures
f. a place that has decayed or been destroyed
g. a priest who prayed for his people
h. offence, guiltiness
i. affliction
j. just, lawful

JUMP-STARTING THE LESSON

11. According to the In Focus story, the Children of Israel had misplaced their _____ in _____ and become _____ with _____ _____.

UNDERSTANDING THE LESSON

12. Because of their sin, the Israelites were held captive in a foreign land for how many years (see Background)?   a. 25   b. 50   c. 60   d. 70

13. What three major Jewish historical events did the book of Ezra record (Introduction of Ezra 9:5–11, 15, More Light on the Text)?

a. _____
b. _____
c. _____

14. Ezra was a direct descendant of the priestly family that included (Ezra 9:5–7, In Depth):

a. _____   c. _____
b. _____   d. _____

15. Ezra had prepared his heart to do what three things (Ezra 9:5–7, In Depth)?

a. _____

b. _____

c. _____

16. List the eight pagan nations from which the nation of Israel had taken wives (Ezra 9:5–7, In Depth). The:

a. _____   e. _____

b. _____   f. _____

c. _____   g. _____

d. _____   h. _____

17. Often when leaders who are to model righteousness go astray, they lead their followers into sin (Ezra 9:5, More Light on the Text).   True   False

18. In spite of Israel's sin, God extended His _____ and _____ to them (Ezra 9:8, In Depth, More Light on the Text).

COMMITTING TO THE WORD

19. Ezra, the priest, did not excuse and separate himself from the people's sin. What principle can believers learn from Ezra's actions (Ezra 9:15, In Depth, More Light on the Text)?

_____

_____

_____

WALKING IN THE WORD

20. Write a prayer asking God to forgive you of your sin.

_____

_____

_____

_____

_____

_____

_____

_____

> *"Then I told them of the hand of my God which was good upon me; as also the king's words that he had spoken unto me. And they said, Let us rise up and build. So they strengthened their hands for this good work"*
> *(Nehemiah 2:18)*

NEHEMIAH: A MOTIVATOR FOR THE PEOPLE

NEHEMIAH 2:5, 11–20

Use with Bible Study Guide 4.

WORDS AND PHRASES

Match the words, phrases, or names with the correct definitions.

1. ____ Artaxerxes
2. ____ Cyrus the Great
3. ____ Hanani
4. ____ Jerusalem

5. ____ Nehemiah
6. ____ Persia
7. ____ reproach
8. ____ Sanballat
9. ____ sepulchres
10. ___ Tobiah

a. the cupbearer to the king and a motivator of his people
b. burying places or graves
c. the Ammonite, who was an enemy of the Children of Israel
d. the emperor who allowed the first group of exiles to return to their homeland
e. He was king of Persia.
f. one of Nehemiah's brethren
g. It is now called Iran.
h. implies disgrace, scorn, or shame
i. God's holy city; the capital of Judah
j. the Horonite, who was an ememy of the Children of Israel

JUMP-STARTING THE LESSON

11. As discussed in the In Focus story and as Georgia recognized, _____ is the first who we should go to when we are faced with a dilemma.

12. According to the In Focus story, the key to Nehemiah's leadership was also his _____ _____ on _____.

UNDERSTANDING THE LESSON

13. The book of Nehemiah is about one man's _____, _____, and _____ to both his _____ and his _____ (Introduction to More Light on the Text).

14. The narrative also demonstrates God's _____ and _____ over man's affairs, when we put all our _____, _____, and _____ into His hands (Introduction to More Light on the Text).

15. According to the Background section, when Nehemiah heard the news of the troubles and problems that Jerusalem and Judah had suffered, what did he do?

_____

16. Nehemiah was born in captivity and had never seen the city of Jerusalem or been there (Nehemiah 2:5, In Depth, More Light on the Text).   True   False

17. Why did Nehemiah take a few men by night and make a survey of the city (Nehemiah 2:11–12, 16, In Depth, More Light on the Text).

_____

_____

_____

18. Nehemiah did not see himself as a member of the suffering community (Nehemiah 2:16, In Depth, More Light on the Text).   True   False

COMMITTING TO THE WORD

19. Fill in the blanks.

"Then _____ told them of the _____ of my _____ which was _____ upon me; as also the _____ _____ that he had spoken unto me. And they said, _____ _____ _____ _____ and _____. So they _____ their _____ for this _____ _____" (Nehemiah 2:18).

WALKING IN THE WORD

20. Do you feel compelled by God to rise up and help rebuild the inner cities of our great country? Why? Why not? If not you, then who?

_____

_____

_____

_____

_____

_____

_____

_____

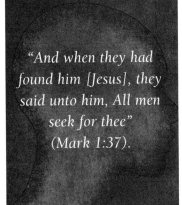

"And when they had found him [Jesus], they said unto him, All men seek for thee" (Mark 1:37).

LOOKING FOR JESUS

MARK 1:35–45

Use with Bible Study Guide 5.

WORDS AND PHRASES

Match the words, phrases, or names with the correct definitions.

1. ____ Capernaum
2. ____ compassion
3. ____ Jehovah Rapha
4. ____ John Mark
5. ____ leper
6. ____ restore
7. ____ solitary

8. ____ the Good News
9. ____ the Good Shepherd
10. ___ untouchables

a. means "the LORD Our Healer"
b. He wrote the second gospel
c. information on how to be saved from sin
d. Jesus
e. outcasts
f. a big city where Jesus taught
g. a person afflicted with a chronic and extremely contagious skin disease
h. sympathy, empathy
i. lonely, desolate, uninhabited
j. to make whole mentally, physically, and spiritually

JUMP-STARTING THE LESSON

11. As cited in the In Focus story, even though some people are not physically healed on this side of heaven, if it is God's will, He can speak the words of _____ and _____.

UNDERSTANDING THE LESSON

12. Scripture shows that there is not always a simple explanation for disease (The People, Places, and Times).   True   False

13. _____ _____ alone is the Son of the _____ _____ (Background).

14. Jesus demonstrated His divinity by overcoming: _____, _____, and even _____ (Background).

15. What did Jesus do to Peter's mother-in-law (Mark 1:35–39, In Depth)?

_____

_____

16. What three things did prayer help Jesus to accomplish (Mark 1:35–37, In Depth, More Light on the Text)?

a. _____

_____

b. _____

_____

c. _____

_____

_____

17. What did the Levitical Law demand when people were stricken with leprosy (Mark 1:40–45, In Depth, More Light on the Text)?

_____

_____

_____

_____

18. When a person asks for and accepts the forgiveness from sin provided by Jesus' crucifixion, that person is _____ _____ _____ (Mark 1:43–44, More Light on the Text).

COMMITTING TO THE WORD

19. Fill in the blanks.

"And _____, moved with _____, put forth _____ _____, and _____ him, and saith unto him, _____ _____; be thou _____ _____" (Mark 1:41).

WALKING IN THE WORD

20. Do you think that everyone who desires physical healing will be healed on this side of heaven? Why or why not? After praying and believing God for healing, if a believer still dies, does that mean that he or she did not have enough faith? Why or why not?

_____

_____

_____

_____

_____

_____

_____

_____

> " *Howbeit Jesus suffered him not, but saith unto him, Go home to thy friends, and tell them how great things the Lord hath done for thee, and hath had compassion on thee*" (Mark 5:19).

RECOGNIZING JESUS

MARK 5:1–13, 18–20

Use with Bible Study Guide 6.

WORDS AND PHRASES

Match the words, phrases, or names with the correct definitions.

1. ____ fetter
2. ____ Decapolis
3. ____ demons
4. ____ Gadara
5. ____ adjure
6. ____ legion
7. ____ swine
8. ____ tomb
9. ____ torment
10. ___ worship

a. charge, plead
b. pigs or hogs
c. to inflict pain, torture, or anguish
d. to bow or to prostrate before a superior; to pay homage
e. something that constrains, a shackle
f. one of the cities of the Decapolis
g. invading evil spirits
h. a federation of ten Greek cities in central Palestine
i. approximately 6,000 Roman soldiers and 726 horsemen
j. grave, sepulchre, burial ground

JUMP-STARTING THE LESSON

11. In the In Focus story, why did Pastor Young dismiss Bryant from his position as director and choir member?

_____

_____

UNDERSTANDING THE LESSON

12. Where had the Gadarene-demonic been living (Mark 5:1–5, In Depth, More Light on the Text)?

_____

13. Why were the people afraid to go near this demon-possessed man (Mark 5:1–5, In Depth, More Light on the Text)? _____

14. When the demonic man saw Jesus in the distance, what did he do (Mark 5:6, In Depth, More Light on the Text)?

_____

15. Satan does not know who Jesus is (Mark 5:6, In Depth, More Light on the Text)?

    True   False

16. When Jesus told the demon to leave the man, the devil immediately receded (Mark 5:9–10, In Depth, More Ligh on the Text).   True   False

17. Healing the Gardarene-demonic demonstrates Jesus' ability to deal with _____ human _____ an _____ (Mark 5:11–13, In Depth, More Light on the Text).

18. The man recognized Jesus as whom (Mark 5:18–19, In Depth, More Light on the Text)?

_____

COMMITTING TO THE WORD

19. The fact that when the Gardarene-demonic first saw Jesus, he worshipped him (Mark 5:6), tells us that when we are seeking deliverance and healing, we should do what?

_____

WALKING IN THE WORD

20. Recall a time when you needed deliverance or healing. Indicate what you did during the experience and why.

_____

_____

_____

_____

_____

_____

_____

_____

"The woman was a Greek, a Syrophenician by nation; and she besought him that he would cast forth the devil out of her daughter" (Mark 7:26).

BEGGING TO GET IN

MARK 7:24–30

Use with Bible Study Guide 7.

WORDS AND PHRASES

Match the words, phrases, or names with the correct definitions.

1. ____ bread
2. ____ devil
3. ____ faith
4. ____ Gentile
5. ____ "mountains"
6. ____ Phoenicia
7. ____ proselyte
8. ____ Syrophenician
9. ____ tenacity
10. ___ Tyre

a. persistence
b. problems, trials, tribulations
c. the name of a mixed race, half Phoenicians and half Syrians
d. territory next to Galilee
e. a Phoenician city on the Mediterranean
f. non-Jew
g. food of any kind
h. a convert
i. a complete confidence, trust, and reliance in and on God
j. evil spirits or messengers and ministers of Satan

JUMP-STARTING THE LESSON

11. According to the In Focus story, Christians have the privilege of being able to _____ to _____ for help in meeting their needs.

12. Jesus _____ reached out to a _____ to restore her daughter's _____ _____.

UNDERSTANDING THE LESSON

13. In the encounter between this Gentile woman and Jesus, we see that our Lord's _____ and _____ know no _____ of _____, _____, or _____ (Background).

14. When the woman begged Jesus to cast out the demon from her daughter, she begged Him for _____ (Mark 7:24–28), In Depth, More Light on the Text).

15. When Jesus answered the woman, "Let the children first be filled", what did He mean (Mark 7:24, In Depth, More Light on the Text)? _____
_____

16. In real spiritual warfare, what four things do we need to fight through for our deliverance or healing (Mark 7:24-28, In Depth, More Light on the Text)?

a. _____

c. _____

b. _____

d. _____

17. When Jesus helped the Syrophenician woman, he demonstrated _____ and _____ for those who are hurting (Mark 7:29–30, In Depth, More Light on the Text)?

18. The Syrophenician woman was begging to get into God's _____ and her _____ got her in (Mark 7:29–30, In Depth, More Light on the Text).

COMMITTING TO THE WORD

19. Memorize, write verbatim, and explain Mark 7:28.

a. _____

_____

_____

_____

b. Explanation:

_____

_____

_____

WALKING IN THE WORD

20. Like the Syrophenician woman, are you willing to beg the Lord, if necessary, for a breakthrough in meetin a grave personal need? Why or why not?

_____

_____

_____

_____

_____

_____

> "Then Jesus beholding him loved him, and said unto him, One thing thou lackest: go thy way, sell whatsoever thou hast, and give to the poor, and thou shalt have treasure in heaven: and come, take up the cross, and follow me" (Mark 10:21).

OPTING OUT!

MARK 10:17–31

Use with Bible Study Guide 8.

WORDS AND PHRASES

Match the words, phrases, or names with the correct definitions.

1. ____ eschatological
2. ____ beholding
3. ____ eternal
4. ____ good
5. ____ "he was sad"
6. ____ "inherit eternal life"
7. ____ security
8. ____ "the day of judgment"
9. ____ the "hundred fold"
10. ___ "the kingdom"

a. to share in the Kingdom of God
b. the royal power of Jesus as the triumphant Messiah
c. trusting in God instead of material wealth
d. without beginning or end, everlasting
e. looking at with the mind; considering
f. excellent, distinguished, upright, honorable
g. Jesus will give back more than what was lost.
h. sorrowful, grieved
i. the study of end times
j. It is marked by Jesus' Second Coming

JUMP-STARTING THE LESSON

11. According to the In Focus story, God wants us to _____ all others and _____ Him.

UNDERSTANDING THE LESSON

12. According to The People, Places, and Times, a "needle's eye" is thought to be:

_____

13. According to the Background section, a wealthy person could relinquish wealth only by _____

_____.

14. Jesus challenged the young man's ideas about _____ (Mark 10:18, In Depth, More Light on the text).

15. Jesus pointed the young man to what he _____ or _____—the _____ of _____, the revealed will of God as expressed in the _____ _____ (Mark 10:19, In Depth, More Light on the Text).

16. Jesus lovingly uncovered the young man's obedience to the law as _____ and challenged him to a deeper level of _____ _____ (Mark 10:20, In Depth, More Light on the Text).

17. Jesus really wanted to help this young man to see _____ what obtaining _____
_____ entailed (Mark 10:21, In Depth, More Light on the Text).

18. Why did the young man go away sad (Mark 10:22, In Depth, More Light on the Text)?
_____
_____

COMMITTING TO THE WORD

19 a. Fill in the blanks and give the meaning of this passage of Scripture.
"And _____ looking upon them saith, With _____ it is _____, but not with
_____: for with _____ _____ things are _____" (Mark 10:27).

b. Explanation:
_____
_____
_____

WALKING IN THE WORD

20. Recall a time in your life when God did the impossible.
_____
_____
_____
_____
_____
_____
_____
_____

"But as he which hath called you is holy, so be ye holy in all manner of conversation; because it is written, BE YE HOLY; FOR I AM HOLY" (1 Peter 1:15–16).

A HOLY PEOPLE

1 PETER 1:13–25

Use with Bible Study Guide 9.

WORDS AND PHRASES

Match the words, phrases, or names with the correct definitions.

1. _____ epistles
2. _____ fear
3. _____ foreordained
4. _____ "gird up the loins of their mind"
5. _____ holy
6. _____ hope
7. _____ "imitate Him"
8. _____ Peter
9. _____ "sinful traditions"
10. _____ "sojourning"

a. set apart from sin
b. one of the 12 disciples; his name means "rock"
c. confident expectation
d. to have determined beforehand
e. beliefs, values, and behavior before salvation
f. dwelling in a strange land
g. reverential awe of God
h. to be alert and sober
i. to follow and obey Christ
j. letters

JUMP-STARTING THE LESSON

11. According to the In Focus story, holiness is the standard requirement for Christians.
True   False

12. According to the In Focus story, believers should _____ and walk in _____. We should be a _____ witness for Him.

UNDERSTANDING THE LESSON

13. Peter was one of Jesus' closest associates, along with _____ and _____ (The People, Places, and Times).

14. The apostle Peter wrote his epistle to believers residing where (Background)?
a. _____   d. _____
b. _____   e. _____
c. _____

15. He wrote this letter to comfort believers who were experiencing great _____ and _____ because of their _____ in the _____ _____ _____ (Background).

16. Peter's letter is a call to _____
(1 Peter 1:13–16, In Depth, More Light on the Text).

17. Who helps believers to live a holy life (1 Peter 1:13–16, In Depth, More Light on the Text)?

_____

_____

18. Peter encourages believers to face our trials and setbacks with a _____ _____ and _____ _____ (1 Peter 1:24–25, More Light on the Text).

COMMITTING TO THE WORD

19 a. Memorize, write verbatim, and explain 1 Peter 1:15–16.

a._____

_____

_____

_____

Explanation:

b._____

_____

_____

WALKING IN THE WORD

20. Why did Peter encourage believers to face our trials and setbacks in a way that honors God? How can we carry out this mandate?

_____

_____

_____

_____

_____

_____

_____

_____

_____

> "But ye are a chosen generation, a royal priesthood, an holy nation, a peculiar people; that ye should shew forth the praises of him who hath called you out of darkness into his marvelous light" (1 Peter 2:9).

A CHOSEN PEOPLE

1 PETER 2:1-10

Use with Bible Study Guide 10.

WORDS AND PHRASES

Match the words, phrases, or names with the correct definitions.

1. _____ "Chief Cornerstone"
2. _____ election
3. _____ envy
4. _____ guile
5. _____ hypocrisy
6. _____ malice
7. _____ mercy
8. _____ sincere
9. _____ "to offer up"
10. ___ unfeigned

a. pure
b. being untruthful
c. ill will toward others
d. sincere, heartfelt
e. to bring to the altar
f. deceptiveness, craftiness, cunning
g. the foundation on which the Christian faith is based—Christ
h. compassion, forgiveness, kindness, sympathy
i. despising another because you want what they have
j. to be chosen by God

JUMP-STARTING THE LESSON

11. According to the In Focus story, God decided before _____ that _____ would _____ the _____ with His _____.

UNDERSTANDING THE LESSON

12. According to The People, Places, and Times, by virtue of God's _____ of the fathers, Israel became God's _____ _____.

13. When God's people live by _____ _____, it changes our _____ (Background).

14. What does "to be born anew" means in terms of eternal salvation (1 Peter 2:1–3, In Depth, More Light on the Text)?

_____
_____

15. Reborn children of God should crave the _____ _____ of God's Word (1 Peter 2:1–3, In Depth, More Light on the Text).

16. a. Instead of being connected to the _____ _____—Jesus—those who disbelieve find Him to be "a _____ of _____. Explain what the foregoing statement means (1 Peter 2:8, In Depth, More Light on the Text).

b. Explanation: _____

_____

_____

17. The _____ is now designated as the _____ of _____, His _____ _____, His _____ _____, His _____ _____, His _____ for His own _____ (1 Peter 2:9, More Light on the Text).

18. Believers are the recipients of God's divine _____ (1 Peter 2:10, More Light on the Text).

COMMITTING TO THE WORD

19 a. Fill in the blanks and explain 1 Peter 2:9.

"But ye are a _____ _____, a _____ _____, an _____ a _____ _____; that ye should shew forth the _____ of _____ wh hath called you _____ of _____ into his marvelous _____" (1 Peter 2:9).

b. Explanation:

_____

_____

_____

WALKING IN THE WORD

20. What does craving the "undiluted (sincere or pure) milk of God's Word" mean to you? Why?

_____

_____

_____

_____

_____

_____

_____

> "Wherefore let them that suffer according to the will of God commit the keeping of their souls to him in well doing, as unto a faithful Creator" (1 Peter 4:19).

A SUFFERING PEOPLE

1 PETER 4:12–19

Use with Bible Study Guide 11.

WORDS AND PHRASES

Match the words, phrases, or names with the correct definitions.

1. ____ "Commit the keeping"
2. ____ "faithfully endure"
3. ____ "fiery trials"
4. ____ glorify
5. ____ Jesus
6. ____ judgment
7. ____ Peter
8. ____ reproach
9. ____ suffer
10. ___ the Holy Spirit

a. to magnify, extol, and praise
b. an apostle, who preached the Gospel wherever he went
c. revile, mock, heap insults upon
d. He enables believers to glorify God, even when suffering.
e. to entrust, commend
f. to endure harm, injury, pain
g. an intense degree of some painful occurrence or experience
h. in suffering, do not give up on your trust in God
i. He was without sin.
j. judicial determination

JUMP-STARTING THE LESSON

11. According to the In Focus story, God guarantees believers freedom from suffering.

True   False

UNDERSTANDING THE LESSON

12. Peter _____ suffered for his _____ in _____ (The People, Places, and Times).

13. _____ and _____ are the main themes of Peter's first letter (Background).

14. Why did Peter instruct Christians to rejoice in their sufferings (Introduction—More Light on the Text).
_____
_____

15. _____ is our example of suffering in _____ (1 Peter 4:12, In Depth).

16. Bringing believers to God or restoring our relationship with God was achieved through Christ's atoning _____ and _____ (1 Peter 4:12, In Depth).

17. When Peter had received the Holy Spirit, he _____, _____, and was _____ for _____ (1 Peter 4:15–19, In Depth, More Light on the Text).

18. According to the apostle Peter, what are three rewards of suffering (1 Peter 4:15–19, In Depth, More Light on the Text).

a. _____
b. _____
c. _____

COMMITTING TO THE WORD

19. Fill in the blanks and then tell what this means to you.
a. According to the apostle Peter, we were created by _____ for His _____ _____ (1 Peter 4:19, More Light on the Text).

b. Explanation: _____
_____
_____

WALKING IN THE WORD

20. List five points from the lesson that you should remember when you are suffering or going through trials and tribulations.

a. _____
b. _____
c. _____
d. _____
e. _____

> "According as his divine power hath given unto us all things that pertain unto life and godliness, through the knowledge of him that hath called us to glory and virtue" (2 Peter 1:3).

A FAITHFUL PEOPLE

2 PETER 1:3–15

Use with Bible Study Guide 12.

WORDS AND PHRASES

Match the words, phrases, or names with the correct definitions.

1. ____ "being diligent"
2. ____ charity
3. ____ epistle
4. ____ godliness
5. ____ James
6. ____ knowledge
7. ____ patience
8. ____ Saul
9. ____ temperance
10. ___ virtue

a. to have discernment or to perceive
b. to wait, abide, endure, or suffer
c. reverence or piety
d. He was one of the primary persecutors of Christians.
e. obedient
f. godly love
g. holy courage, strength
h. letter
i. an apostle, the brother of John, who was put to death by Herod Agrippa I
j. self control; holding passions in control

JUMP-STARTING THE LESSON

11. According to the In Focus story, faith is equivalent to blind optimism.   True   False

UNDERSTANDING THE LESSON

12. After the death of _____, His _____ became objects of _____ and _____ (The People, Places, and Times).

13. After _____, many believers were _____, _____, and _____ (The People, Places, and Times).

14. The apostle Peter knew that it was only through an _____ _____ with and _____ _____ of _____ and of _____ _____, _____ _____ that believers might experience God's grace and peace (Background).

15. When we are born into the family of God by _____ in _____, we are born _____ (2 Peter 1:3, More Light on the Text).

16. We should reveal God's beauty and grace in our _____ and _____, (2 Peter 1:3, More Light on the Text).

17. If we live as God wants us to, He promises us an _____ life and _____ into His _____ (2 Peter 1:11, In Depth, More Light on the Text).

18. After his death, what was it that Peter left behind (2 Peter 1:13, In Depth, More Light on the Text).

_____

_____

COMMITTING TO THE WORD

19. Memorize 2 Peter 1:3, write it verbatim, and explain.

a. _____

_____

_____

_____

b. Explanation:

_____

_____

_____

WALKING IN THE WORD

20. Explain why believers should show agape (Godly love) to even their enemies.

_____

_____

_____

_____

_____

_____

_____

> *"The Lord is not slack concerning his promise, as some men count slackness; but is longsuffering to usward, not willing that any should perish, but that all should come to repentance"* (2 Peter 3:9).

A HOPEFUL PEOPLE

2 PETER 3:1–13

Use with Bible Study Guide 13.

WORDS AND PHRASES

Match the words, phrases, or names with the correct definitions.

1. _____ apostle
2. _____ "a promise"
3. _____ lust
4. _____ perdition
5. _____ repentance
6. _____ scoffer
7. _____ the "Day of the Lord"
8. _____ "the firmament"
9. _____ "the last days"
10. _____ "to stir up"

a. to fully awaken
b. the massive transparent dome that covers the earth
c. one who ridicules, mocks, or makes fun of others
d. the period between the first and second coming of Christ
e. a messenger, envoy
f. a binding declaration between two or more parties
g. destruction, annihilation, ruin
h. a strong desire for something forbidden
i. a change of mind, a turning around in one's life
j. the occasion when God will judge sin and the world

JUMP-STARTING THE LESSON

11. According to the In Focus story, the apostle Peter confirms Christ's promise to _____ and usher in the _____ _____ and _____ _____.

UNDERSTANDING THE LESSON

12. Name two important reasons why the apostle Peter wrote 2 Peter 3:1–13 (Background).

a. _____

b. _____

13. Peter did not want the recipients of the letter to forget the things he had _____ them or become _____ in their _____ with _____ (2 Peter 3:1, In Depth, More Light on the Text).

14. Scoffers do not believe the _____ of _____ _____ (2 Peter 3:5–9, In Depth, More Light on the Text).

15. The _____ of sin has _____ the _____ and the _____ (2 Peter 3:5–9, In Depth, More Light on the Text).

16. When Peter declares that the Earth will be burned up and the works that are therein, he means that _____ that _____ has ever _____, _____, or _____ will be utterly _____ in the "fervent heat" (2 Peter 3:10–13, In Depth, More Light on the Text).

17. The "Day of the Lord" is portrayed as a day of _____ and _____ for the _____ and _____ of God and Israel (2 Peter 2:10–13, In Depth, More Light on the Text).

18. How is the "Day of the Lord" described in Matthew 24 (2 Peter 2:10–13, In Depth, More Light on the Text)?

_____

_____

_____

_____

COMMITTING TO THE WORD

19a. Write 2 Peter 3:9 verbatim and explain its meaning.

_____

_____

_____

b. Explanation:

_____

_____

_____

WALKING IN THE WORD

20. Are you prepared for Jesus' Second Coming? Why? Why not?

_____

_____

_____

_____

_____

_____

"And the women her neighbours gave it a name, saying, There is a son born to Naomi; and they called his name Obed: he is the father of Jesse, the father of David"
(Ruth 4:17)

THE LINEAGE OF DAVID

RUTH 4:13–17; MATTHEW 1:1–6

Use with Bible Study Guide 1.

WORDS AND PHRASES

Match the words, phrases, or names with the correct definitions.

1. _____ "begat"
2. _____ Boaz
3. _____ Elimelech
4. _____ Jesse
5. _____ "Jehoshua"
6. _____ Obed
7. _____ Orpah
8. _____ origin
9. _____ Rahab
10. ___ Ruth

a. Naomi's devoted daughter-in-law
b. a Hebrew name for "Jesus" that means "Jehovah is Savior"
c. the grandfather of Israel's greatest king, David
d. expresses the conformity of a son to his father
e. the father of Israel's greatest king, David
f. Naomi's daughter-in-law who went back to her own people
g. the prostitute who became the mother of Boaz
h. a relative of Naomi, and a wealthy land owner
i. Naomi's dead son, who had been married to Ruth
j. birth, beginning

JUMP-STARTING THE LESSON

11. According to the In Focus story, Lydia discovered that real freedom requires _____.

12. According to the In Focus story, by _____ her life to _____, she was _____ from the _____ of _____.

UNDERSTANDING THE LESSON

13. According to The People, Places, and Times, _____ was a _____ woman and Israelites were _____ to marry them.

14. Who were Naomi's two daughters-in-law (see Background)? a. _____ b. _____

15. Ruth was a _____ and _____ were _____ and descendants of _____ (Ruth 4:13–14, In Depth, More Light on the Text).

16. How many generations are there between Abraham and the birth of Jesus (Matthew 1:1–6, In Depth, More Light on the Text)?

a. 12   b. 32   c. 42   d. 52   e. 62

17. _____ is the father of _____, the father of _____ (Ruth 4:17, In Depth, Mo
Light on the Text).

18. Who are the two most important names in the genealogy of Jesus (Matthew 1-6, In Depth, More Light o
the Text)? a. _____ b. _____

COMMITTING TO THE WORD

19. Who were the four women in Jesus' genealogy, whose lives were not above reproach? Tell what they did
were known for that was not above reproach and then fill in the blank (Matthew 1:6, More Light on the Tex
a. _____, who was an _____
b. _____, who was an _____
c. _____, who was a _____
d. _____, who was an _____.

They all found _____ in the eyes of the _____ and became a part of His plan for the
_____ of the whole world.

WALKING IN THE WORD

20. Explain what the "grace" of God toward mankind means to and for you.

_____

_____

_____

_____

_____

_____

_____

_____

"Therefore the Lord himself shall give you a sign; Behold, a virgin shall conceive, and bear a son, and shall call his name Immanuel" (Isaiah 7:14).

PROPHETS FORESHADOW MESSIAH'S BIRTH

ISAIAH 7:13–17; LUKE 1:30–38

Use with Bible Study Guide 2.

WORDS AND PHRASES

Match the words, phrases, or names with the correct definitions.

1. ____ angel
2. ____ "butter and honey"
3. ____ Elizabeth
4. ____ Gabriel
5. ____ "house of David"
6. ____ Immanuel
7. ____ Jesus
8. ____ prophet
9. ____ Shear-Jashub
10. ___ virgin

a. the angel who appeared to Mary with the news of her pregnancy
b. The word means "messenger."
c. the prophet Isaiah's young son
d. means "the Lord saves"
e. a young woman of marriageable age, but not yet married
f. a speaker of or for God
g. means "God with us"
h. refers to the royal family
i. They express abundance.
j. Mary's cousin, who was also pregnant

JUMP-STARTING THE LESSON

11. According to the In Focus story, God rarely sends a prophet or an angel to speak to us today because we can listen to Him speaking to us through _____ _____.

12. According to the In Focus story, God speaks to us through the _____ in the midst of our _____ _____.

UNDERSTANDING THE LESSON

13. When He led the Israelites out of slavery and when He gave Moses the Ten Commandments, God spoke to Moses face to face (The People, Places, and Times).   True   False

14. The appearance of angels is often in _____ _____ _____ (The People, Places, and Times).

15. According to the Bible, where do human beings rank in relations to angels (The People, Places, and Times)? _____
_____

16. God knew that King Ahaz had very little _____ and so God asked Ahaz if he would like a _____ to verify the _____ of this _____.

17. Why is the virgin birth important to our salvation (Luke 1:30–38, In Depth, More Light on the Text)?

_____

_____

_____

_____

_____

18. In Luke 1:32, what did the angel mean by "the boy will be great"?

_____

_____

_____

_____

_____

COMMITTING TO THE WORD

19. "Therefore the _____ himself shall give you a _____; Behold a _____ shall _____, and bear a _____, and shall call his name _____" (Isaiah 7:14).

WALKING IN THE WORD

20. What does the statement "God with us" mean in your own personal life?

_____

_____

_____

_____

_____

_____

_____

_____

"And she shall bring forth a son, and thou shalt call his name JESUS: for he shall save his people from their sins" (Matthew 1:21).

EMMANUEL IS BORN

MATTHEW 1:18–25

Use with Bible Study Guide 3.

WORDS AND PHRASES

Match the words, phrases, or names with the correct definitions.

1. _____ Emmanuel or Immanuel
2. _____ espoused
3. _____ genesis
4. _____ God
5. _____ Jesus
6. _____ Joseph
7. _____ "knew her not"
8. _____ Mary
9. _____ Nazareth
10. ___ virgin

a. a descendant of King David and Jesus' earthly father
b. denotes origin or beginning
c. means "Yahweh is Saviour"
d. the mother of Jesus
e. interpreted as "God with us"
f. a promise to be married, betrothed
g. one's marriageable daughter
h. the city where Joseph was born
i. Jesus' Father
j. "did not have sexual intercourse with her"

JUMP-STARTING THE LESSON

11. According to the In Focus story, our _____ _____ sent His one and only _____ to be with us.

12. According to the In Focus story, "He came to _____, _____, and _____ us as well and He will never _____ or _____ us.

UNDERSTANDING THE LESSON

13. The Book of Matthew is called the "_____ _____" because its intended audience is _____ (see Background).

14. Jesus was conceived by the _____ _____ (see Background).

15a. The _____ _____ of _____ is crucial to Christianity. Why (Matthew 1:18, In Depth, More Light on the Text)?

b. _____
_____
_____

16. Because _____ was Jesus' Father, Jesus was born with the characteristics of _____ (Matthew 1:18, In Depth, More Light on the Text).

17. Joseph and Mary's story shows us that sometimes God will lead us into situations that bring hardship, embarrassment, and humiliation into our lives (Matthew 1:20, In Depth, More Light on the Text).
True   False

18. Jesus' birth is a _____ of the _____ _____ (Matthew 1:22, I Depth, More Light on the Text).

COMMITTING TO THE WORD
19. Fill in the blanks.
"And she shall _____ a _____, and thou shalt call his name
_____: for he shall _____ from their _____"
(Matthew 1:21).

WALKING IN THE WORD
20. Write a prayer thanking God for Jesus and for saving you from your sins. If you are not saved, ask Him to save you.

_____

_____

_____

_____

_____

_____

_____

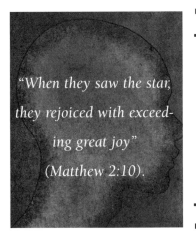

"When they saw the star, they rejoiced with exceeding great joy" (Matthew 2:10).

MAGI CONFIRM MESSIAH'S BIRTH

MATTHEW 2:7–9, 16–23

Use with Bible Study Guide 4.

WORDS AND PHRASES

Match the words, phrases, or names with the correct definitions.

1. ____ Antipas
2. ____ Archelaus
3. ____ Bethlehem
4. ____ Herod
5. ____ Magi
6. ____ mock
7. ____ Nazareth
8. ____ Persia
9. ____ wise men
10. ___ worship

a. Jesus' hometown; Mary and Joseph returned to live with Jesus there.
b. the Latin word for "wise men"
c. Herod's son, who was made ruler of Galilee
d. the place where Jesus was predicted to be born
e. to adore, to reverence, to bow down to
f. one skilled in oriental astrology, a magician, a sorcerer
g. Herod's evil son
h. one of the cruelest rulers in all of history
i. to make a fool of
j. modern day Iran

JUMP-STARTING THE LESSON

11. According to the In Focus story, why did Kathy's tour of Egypt make her feel even closer to Jesus?

_____

_____

_____

12. According to the In Focus story, the wise men traveled many miles seeking _____ _____

_____.

UNDERSTANDING THE LESSON

13. Matthew 2 opens with _____ _____ coming from the _____ in search of the _____ _____ of the Jews (Background).

14. Compare the three different responses (Herod, Bible scholars, and the wise men) to Jesus (Matthew 2:7–9, In Depth, More Light on the Text).

a. Herod: _____

b. Bible scholars: _____

c. the wise men: _____

15. When the wise men finally found Jesus, He was what age (Matthew 2:16–18, In Depth, More Light on the Text)?   a. one   b. two   c. three   d. four   e. five

16. How did Herod respond to the wise men not returning with the information on where the baby Jesus was (Matthew 2:16–18, In Depth, More Light on the Text)?

_____

_____

_____

_____

_____

_____

17. List two reasons why the star that the wise men saw reappeared (Matthew 2:7-9, In Depth, More Light on the Text).
a. _____

_____

b. _____

_____

18. What does Matthew 2:18 mean: "In Rama was there a voice heard, lamentation, and weeping, and great mourning, Rachel weeping for her children, and would not be comforted, because they are not"?

_____

_____

_____

COMMITTING TO THE WORD
19. Fill in the blanks.
"When they saw the _____, they _____ with _____ _____
_____" (Matthew 2:10).

WALKING IN THE WORD
20. Do you desire a closer relationship with Jesus? Why? Why not?

_____

_____

_____

_____

_____

_____

_____

_____

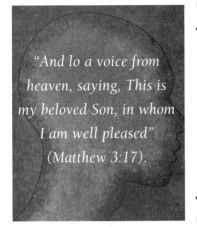

"And lo a voice from heaven, saying, This is my beloved Son, in whom I am well pleased" (Matthew 3:17).

PROCLAIMED IN BAPTISM

MATTHEW 3:1–6, 11–17

Use with Bible Study Guide 5.

WORDS AND PHRASES

Match the words, phrases, or names with the correct definitions.

1. ____ baptism
2. ____ chaff
3. ____ John the Baptist
4. ____ Jordan River
5. ____ Judean Wilderness
6. ____ preaching
7. ____ repent
8. ____ sin
9. ____ Spirit
10. ___ wilderness

a. a voice shouting in the wilderness
b. proclaiming a message
c. an offense against God's Law
d. a turning from self to God
e. It emphasizes repentance leading to a changed life.
f. It means "breath"; "the third person of the Trinity."
g. husk or other useless materials separated from grain
h. desert
i. It is between the Sea of Galilee and the Dead Sea.
j. It was located not far from the Dead Sea.

JUMP-STARTING THE LESSON

11. As cited in the In Focus story, what things can you point out in Scripture to encourage someone to get baptized? _____

_____

12. Jesus showed _____ and _____ to God when He came to John for _____, and John the Baptist showed _____ to _____ (In Focus story).

UNDERSTANDING THE LESSON

13. The people had not heard from a _____ since the days of Malachi, but when they saw and heard _____, they recognized him as a _____ (Matthew 3:1–6, In Depth, More Light on the Text).

14. John pointed out _____, so that people could _____. Without _____, people cannot receive _____ into their _____ (Matthew 3:1–6, In Depth, More Light on the Text).

15. List eight similarities between John the Baptist and Jesus (Matthew 3:2, More Light on the Text).

a. _____

b. _____

c. _____

d. _____

e. _____

f. _____

g. _____

h. _____

16. Name two things that John the Baptist foretold (Matthew 3:11–12, In Depth, More Light on the Text):

a. _____

b. _____

17. The word "Trinity" never appears in Scripture (Matthew 3:13–17, In Depth, More Light on the Text).
True   False

18. List the three members of the Trinity (Matthew 3:13–17, In Depth, More Light on the Text):

a. _____   b. _____   c. _____   _____

COMMITTING TO THE WORD

19a. Fill in the blanks and explain the Scripture.

"And lo a voice from _____, saying, _____, in whom am _____" (Matthew 3:17).

b. Explanation: _____

_____

_____

_____

WALKING IN THE WORD

20. According to our Scripture discussion, how was Jesus proclaimed in baptism and how are you proclaimed in baptism? Have you been baptized? Why? Why not?

_____

_____

_____

> "Then saith Jesus unto him, Get thee hence, Satan: for it is written, THOU SHALT WORSHIP THE LORD THY GOD, AND HIM ONLY SHALT THOU SERVE" (Matthew 4:10).

STRENGTHENED IN TEMPTATION

MATTHEW 4:1–11

Use with Bible Study Guide 6.

WORDS AND PHRASES

Match the words, phrases, or names with the correct definitions.

1. ____ devil
2. ____ fasting
3. ____ Jerusalem
4. ____ "Jesus' passion"
5. ____ manna
6. ____ pinnacle
7. ____ tempt
8. ____ the kingdom of God
9. ____ the presence of God
10. ___ the Spirit

a. to test thoroughly
b. the reign of the Master
c. points to the reality of God
d. a high point
e. known as the tempter, false accuser, slanderer
f. "the holy city"
g. bread; food from heaven
h. means not eating; seeking God's guidance
i. the Third Person of the Trinity
j. Jesus' suffering before dying on the Cross

JUMP-STARTING THE LESSON

11. As mentioned in the In Focus story, list three ways that we can fight against temptations.

a. _____

b. _____

c. _____

UNDERSTANDING THE LESSON

12. According to The People, Places, and Times, Satan may appear as an _____ of _____, but he is actually a _____ _____.

13. Immediately after Jesus was baptized, the _____ led Him into the _____ where He fasted for _____ days and _____ nights (Background).

14. Fasting is more than a physical discipline (Background).   True   False

15. Fasting is something that can be used to manipulate God (Background).   True   False

16. List three situations in which fasting can be used (Background):

a. _____

_____

b. _____

_____

c. _____

_____

17. Jesus withstood the human temptations of _____, _____, and _____ (Matthew 4:1–11; More Light on the Text).

18. In the three temptations, what did Jesus use each time to combat the devil (Matthew 4:4, 7, 10; In Depth; More Light on the Text)?

COMMITTING TO THE WORD

Fill in the blanks.

19. "Then saith Jesus unto him, _____ _____ _____, _____; for it is _____, Thou shalt _____ the _____ thy _____, and _____ _____ shalt thou _____" (Matthew 4:10).

WALKING IN THE WORD

20. Share a time when you were in the presence of the Lord and were tempted by Satan shortly after your encounter with God. How did you handle the situation?

_____

_____

_____

_____

_____

_____

_____

_____

> "The blind receive their sight, and the lame walk, the lepers are cleansed, and the deaf hear, the dead are raised up, and the poor have the gospel preached to them" (Matthew 11:5).

DEMONSTRATED IN ACTS OF HEALING

MATTHEW 9:27–34; 11:2–6

Use with Bible Study Guide 7.

WORDS AND PHRASES

Match the words, phrases, or names with the correct definitions.

1. ____ blessed
2. ____ faith
3. ____ follow
4. ____ Galilee
5. ____ John the Baptist
6. ____ King Herod
7. ____ Matthew
8. ____ mercy
9. ____ mystery
10. ____ Theocentric

a. to have or receive compassion or aid
b. Levi, a Jewish tax collector who became one of Jesus' disciples
c. when people cannot explain events
d. God–centered
e. happy
f. to believe with trust that Jesus is the Messiah; believe the truth
g. It is located in the northern part of Palestine.
h. to join or accompany as a disciple
i. He placed John the Baptist in jail because he told him the truth.
j. preached a message of repentance in the wilderness

JUMP-STARTING THE LESSON

11. According to the In Focus story, the two blind men were healed by their statement of _____.

12. When we need help or feel discouraged, we must _____ our _____, _____, and _____, who is _____ _____.

UNDERSTANDING THE LESSON

13. Before Jesus actually came, for more than how many years did the prophets foretell of His coming (Background)?

a. 100   b. 200   c. 300   d. 400   e. 500

14. What kind of leader were the Jews looking for and why (Background)?

_____

_____

_____

15. The Old Testament foretold of a _____ _____ who _____ for the sins of all _____ (Background).

_____

16. The apostle Matthew wrote his gospel to the
_____ (Background).

17. Why was healing an important part of Jesus' ministry (Matthew 9:29–31, In Depth, More Light on the Text)?

_____

_____

_____

_____

_____

_____

18. Name three parts of Jesus' ministry (Matthew 11:2–6, In Depth, More Light on the Text).

a. _____

_____

b. _____

_____

c. _____

COMMITTING TO THE WORD
19. Memorize, write verbatim, and explain Matthew 11:5.

a. _____

_____

_____

_____

b. Explanation:

_____

_____

_____

_____

WALKING IN THE WORD
20. List some ways that you can show your faith in action to those around you.

_____

_____

_____

_____

_____

_____

_____

> *"Come unto me, all ye that labour and are heavy laden, and I will give you rest"*
> *(Matthew 11:28)*

DECLARED IN PRAYER

Use with Bible Study Guide 8.

WORDS AND PHRASES

Match the words, phrases, or names with the correct definitions.

1. _____ Bethsaida   a. the commands of Jesus Christ
2. _____ Capernaum   b. to uncover
3. _____ Chorazin   c. Jesus
4. _____ Pharisees   d. a small Jewish village in northern Galilee
5. _____ prayer   e. the home base to Jesus' ministry
6. _____ reveal   f. a fishing village located east of the Jordan River
7. _____ The Kingdom   g. Jewish religious leaders whose name means "separated ones."
8. _____ The Father   h. the reign of the Almighty
9. _____ The Son   i. a form of communicating with God
10. ___ yoke   j. God

JUMP-STARTING THE LESSON

11. According to the In Focus story, prayer is the opportunity to _____ with _____

through _____.

12. According to the In Focus story, what are four things included in our communications with God?

a. _____   b. _____

c. _____   d. _____

UNDERSTANDING THE LESSON

13. Jesus taught the truth about the Kingdom of God with God's _____ and
_____ (Background).

14. After revealing many miracles and preaching about the Kingdom of God, Jesus pronounced a direct
_____ on _____ (Background).

15. Where is the truth of God's Kingdom found (Matthew 11:25, In Depth, More Light on the Text)?

_____

16. God reveals the great mysteries of life according to _____ _____ (Matthew 11:26–27, In Depth, More Light on the Text).

17. When we follow Jesus, where does a change begin (Matthew 11:28-30, In Depth, More Light on the Text)? _____

18. As Christians, Jesus' yoke requires that we study the Word of God and practice what three things (Matthew 11:28-30, In Depth, More Light on the Text)? Show: (a) _____, (b)_____, and (c) _____.

COMMITTING TO THE WORD

19a. Fill in the blanks and give the meaning of this passage of Scripture.
"All things are _____ unto _____: and no man knoweth the _____, but the _____; neither knoweth any man the _____, save the _____, and he to whomsoever the _____ will _____ _____" (Matthew 11:27).

b. Explanation:

_____

_____

_____

WALKING IN THE WORD

20. Write a prayer giving a concern to God.

_____

_____

_____

_____

_____

_____

_____

_____

_____

REVEALED IN REJECTION

MATTHEW 13:54–58

> "And he [Jesus] did not do many mighty works there because of their unbelief" (Matthew 13:58).

Use with Bible Study Guide 9.

WORDS AND PHRASES

Match the words, phrases, or names with the correct definitions.

1. ____ Bethlehem
2. ____ "depend on"
3. ____ Isaiah
4. ____ King of kings
5. ____ Messiah
6. ____ Nazareth
7. ____ offended
8. ____ rejection
9. ____ works
10. ___ unbelief

a. means "branch"; a city in lower Galilee
b. the lack of faith or trust
c. refusal, denial, rebuff
d. Jesus
e. strength, power, and ability
f. to have trust in, faith in
g. means "house of bread"; a city southwest of Jerusalem
h. a stumbling block or impediment in the way, scandalized
i. one of the greatest prophets in the Old Testament
j. means "Lord," "Savior," and "King"

JUMP-STARTING THE LESSON

11. According to the In Focus story, even when we feel rejected, we should follow Jesus.

True   False

12. According to the In Focus story, our response to rejection should be to _____ _____, who is _____ (in control of His universe and never out of control).

UNDERSTANDING THE LESSON

13. Jesus preached the _____ of _____ as He revealed the _____ of _____ (Background).

14. When Matthew wrote his gospel, he provided a detailed record of Jesus' _____ to _____ that Jesus is the _____, the _____ (Background).

15. After leaving _____, Jesus crossed the Sea of _____ and went to _____ (Matthew 13:54, In Depth).

16. There had to be at least how many married Jewish men for a synagogue to be established in any town (Matthew 13:54, In Depth, More Light on the Text)?

a. 1   b. 5   c. 7   d. 9   e. 10   f. 12

17. When Jesus revealed amazing wisdom and mighty works, the people were not surprised (Matthew 13:54, In Depth, More Light on the Text).

True   False

18. When Jesus' family and townspeople rejected Him, what was Jesus' reply (Matthew 13:57-57, In Depth, More Light on the Text)?

_____

_____

_____

COMMITTING TO THE WORD

19a. What kept Jesus from doing "many mighty works" for the people of Nazareth (Matthew 13:57–58, In Depth, More Light on the Text)?

_____

b. Explain a time when you had the same response to Jesus in your own life.

_____

_____

_____

_____

WALKING IN THE WORD

20. Share a time in your life when you were rejected by a loved one or a fellow brother or sister in the church? How did you feel? What did you do?

_____

_____

_____

_____

_____

_____

"Then Jesus answered and said unto her, O woman great is thy faith: be it unto thee even as thou wilt. And her daughter was made whole from that very hour" (Matthew 15:28).

RECOGNIZED BY A CANAANITE WOMAN

MATTHEW 15:21–28

Use with Bible Study Guide 10.

WORDS AND PHRASES

Match the words, phrases, or names with the correct definitions.

1. _____ Canaanites
2. _____ Capernaum
3. _____ coasts
4. _____ dogs
5. _____ "made whole"
6. _____ mercy
7. _____ persistent prayer
8. _____ Sidon
9. _____ "Son of David"
10. _____ "worship"

a. the first city founded by the Phoenicians
b. to heal, cure or restore to physical, spiritual, or mental health
c. a title for the Messiah
d. the setting for the first miracle to a Gentile
e. the Black Hamatic people, who originally inhabited Palestine
f. "to bend the knee toward"
g. borders or limits of a country
h. the outward manifestation of pity
i. it is evidence of great faith
j. used by the Jews to describe everyone outside their covenant relationship with God

JUMP-STARTING THE LESSON

11. According to the In Focus story, Jesus hears the prayers of a _____ _____ and meets her at her _____ of _____.

UNDERSTANDING THE LESSON

12. Because of their covenant relationship with God, the Israelites considered themselves distinct and different from all other people (The People, Places, and Times).   True   False

13. Before healing the servant, Jesus heard the Roman centurion's words and was astonished because He had not found anyone in Israel with what (Background)?

_____

14. In the Jewish mindset, contact with Gentiles was one of the things that made a person _____ (Matthew 15:21–23, In Depth, More Light on the Text).

15. Upon seeing Jesus, what did the Syrophenecian woman cry out to Him (Matthew 15:21–23, In Depth, More Light on the Text)? _____

16. Persistent prayer expresses the desires of our _____ in constantly _____ ____ to the _____ for _____ (Matthew 15:21–23, In Depth, More Light on the Text).

17. The two brightest examples of faith seen in Christ's ministry were exhibited by Gentiles who came to Christ to receive their own healing (Matthew 15:28, More Light on the Text).
True   False

18. Prayer can _____ and _____ us from the _____ one (Matthew 15:28, More Light on the Text).

COMMITTING TO THE WORD
19a. Fill in the blanks.
"Then _____ answered and said unto _____,
O _____ _____ is thy _____:
be it unto thee _____ as thou _____. And her _____ was made _____
from that very _____" (Matthew 15:28).

b. Explain Matthew 15:28.
_____
_____
_____

WALKING IN THE WORD
20. Share a time when you desperately went to God and He met you at your point of need.
_____
_____
_____
_____
_____
_____
_____

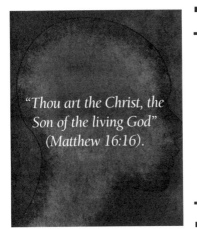

"Thou art the Christ, the Son of the living God" (Matthew 16:16).

DECLARED BY PETER

MATTHEW 16:13–27

Use with Bible Study Guide 11.

WORDS AND PHRASES

Match the words, phrases, or names with the correct definitions.

1. _____ "Barjona"
2. _____ blessed
3. _____ Elijah
4. _____ Jeremiah
5. _____ Jerusalem
6. _____ "keys to the kingdom"
7. _____ "prevail against"
8. _____ rebuke
9. _____ rock
10. _____ savourest

a. to be superior in strength; to overcome
b. to admonish sharply; a chiding or reproof
c. privileged or favored by God
d. the "city of Peace"; the capital of the kingdoms of Israel
e. "son of Jonah"
f. The book of Malachi said that God would send him.
g. firm and unchanging
h. to think, regard, or be like-minded
i. an invitation; a call to salvation
j. His book was placed first in the book of prophecy.

JUMP-STARTING THE LESSON

11. According to the In Focus story, once we affirm that Jesus is our Lord and Savior, we need to go on to declare our allegiance to Him in our everyday living.
True   False

UNDERSTANDING THE LESSON

12. Matthew wrote his gospel for his fellow _____ to prove that Jesus is the _____ and to reveal God's _____ (Background).

13. Part of the prophetic message about Jesus proclaimed that this king would be _____, _____, and named the "_____ _____" (Background).

14. In order to differentiate between a counterfeit or false doctrine and God's Word, we must be _____ in the _____ (Matthew 16:13–19, In Depth).

15. Name eight different roles that Jesus fills in our lives (Matthew 16:13–19, In Depth).
a. _____   b. _____   c. _____
d. _____   e. _____   f. _____
g. _____   h. _____

16. The apostle Peter is the "rock" on which God built His church (Matthew 16:13–19, In Depth).

True   False

17. Jesus was—and is—the only person ever born the Son of God (Matthew 16:13-19, In Depth).

True   False

18. Name four things that being a true follower of Christ requires (Matthew 16:24–27, More Light on the Text).

a. _____

b. _____

c. _____

d. _____

COMMITTING TO THE WORD

19. Fill in the blanks and then tell what this means to you.

a. "And ____ will _____ unto _____ the _____ to the _____ of

_____: and whatsoever _____ shalt _____ on _____ shall be _____ ir

_____: and whatsoever _____ shalt _____ on _____ shall be

_____ in _____" (Matthew 16:19, In Depth, More Light on the Text).

b. Explanation: _____

_____

_____

WALKING IN THE WORD

20. List four points from the lesson that you should remember about Peter's confession of faith. Then answer the follow-ing questions: Who do you say Jesus is? Why?

a. _____

b. _____

c. _____

d. _____

Jesus is: _____

_____

_____

_____

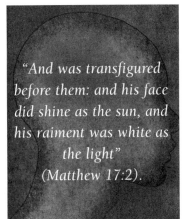

"And was transfigured before them: and his face did shine as the sun, and his raiment was white as the light" (Matthew 17:2).

WITNESSED BY DISCIPLES

MATTHEW 17:1–12

Use with Bible Study Guide 12.

WORDS AND PHRASES

Match the words, phrases, or names with the correct definitions.

1. _____ Elijah
2. _____ "great trial"
3. _____ magnify
4. _____ "mountaintop experience"
5. _____ overshadow
6. _____ Peter
7. _____ scribes
8. _____ tabernacle
9. _____ transfigured
10. ____ vision

a. tent, booth
b. uplift the name of
c. to envelop; to cover
d. He was carried bodily to heaven in a whirlwind.
e. to change in appearance; to change in form
f. something seen
g. He declared Jesus to be the Messiah.
h. caught up in the very presence of God
i. suffering
j. men learned in the Mosaic Law and in the sacred writings; teachers, interpreters

JUMP-STARTING THE LESSON

11. According to the In Focus story, what did God's presence confirm?

_____

_____

UNDERSTANDING THE LESSON

12. Jesus predicted His own _____ and _____ (Background).

13. In Matthew 17, the glory of God was unveiled and _____ in _____ _____ (Background).

14. Name three disciples who were in Jesus' inner circle (Matthew 17:1–5, In Depth, More Light on the Text).
a. _____   b. _____   c. _____

15. Jesus' transfiguration showed the great _____ and _____ of Jesus Christ (Matthew 17:2, In Depth, More Light on the Text).

16. In Matthew 17:3, Moses and Elias appeared to the disciples and talked with Jesus. Moses represented the _____ and Elias, the _____ (In Depth, More Light on the Text).

17. In Matthew 17:7, Jesus comforted His disciples with the tenderness of His _____ (In Depth, More Light on the Text).

18. All direct manifestations from heaven inspire _____ in _____ humanity (Matthew 17:8, In Depth, More Light on the Text).

COMMITTING TO THE WORD

19. Memorize Matthew 17:2, write it verbatim, and explain.

a. _____

_____

_____

b. Explanation:

_____

_____

_____

WALKING IN THE WORD

20. Share a time when you felt that you were in the very presence of Almighty God.

_____

_____

_____

_____

_____

_____

_____

"Verily I say unto you, Wheresoever this gospel shall be preached in the whole world, there shall also this, that this woman hath done, be told for a memorial of her" (Matthew 26:13).

ANOINTED BY A WOMAN IN BETHANY

MATTHEW 26:6–13

Use with Bible Study Guide 13.

WORDS AND PHRASES

Match the words, phrases, or names with the correct definitions.

1. ____ "alabaster box"
2. ____ anointed
3. ____ Bethany
4. ____ covenanted
5. ____ Gospel
6. ____ Judas
7. ____ poor
8. ____ precious
9. ____ provoked
10. ___ work

a. the Good News of God's salvation
b. the person who championed the criticism against Mary
c. beggars
d. to make or establish with a binding agreement or oath
e. the home of Martha, Mary, and Lazarus
f. performance or result of labor
g. rubbed or smeared
h. an expensive container
i. of heavy value
j. incensed, angered

JUMP-STARTING THE LESSON

11. According to the In Focus story, in order for the baby to survive, the mother had to give a _____ _____ of her time, services, etc.

12. According to the In Focus story, the woman in Bethany also chose to give _____ out of her _____ for someone very special: Jesus.

UNDERSTANDING THE LESSON

13. The religious leaders were determined to _____ Jesus at _____ _____, no matter what they had to do (Background).

14. Jesus knew the time of His _____ and _____ would come after the _____ of the _____ (Background).

15. Matthew puts the event of the woman anointing Jesus with perfume at just before the _____ _____ (Background).

16. Matthew does not tell us that it was indeed Judas who championed or instigated this criticism of what woman from Bethany had done (Matthew 26:8, In Depth, More Light on the Text).   True   False

17. We need _____ so that we will not call "_____" what the Lord, Himself, call "_____" (Matthew 26:10, In Depth, More Light on the Text).

18. Jesus explained the deeper significance of this woman's action: "she did it for my _____ (Matthew 26:12, In Depth, More Light on the Text).

COMMITTING TO THE WORD

19a. Write Matthew 26:13 verbatim.

_____

_____

_____

b. Explain what the verse means.

_____

_____

_____

WALKING IN THE WORD

20. Explain in your own words the significance of the woman in Bethany anointing Jesus and what it means to y

_____

_____

_____

_____

_____

_____

_____

_____

_____

> "The people of Nineveh believed God; they proclaimed a fast, and everyone, great and small, put on sackcloth" (Jonah 3:5).

MISSION TO THE COMMUNITY

JONAH 1:1–3; 3:1–9

Use with Bible Study Guide 1.

WORDS AND PHRASES

Match the words, phrases, or names with the correct definitions.

1. ____ a decree
2. ____ fast
3. ____ Jonah
4. ____ Nineveh
5. ____ omniscient
6. ____ proclaim
7. ____ sackcloth
8. ____ sovereign
9. ____ Tarshish
10. ___ throne

a. the city where Jonah went to try to escape God's presence
b. to call or call out
c. worn in mourning or humiliation
d. in control of
e. any elevated seat occupied by a person in authority
f. a judgment, command, declaration
g. to abstain from food and water (or just water)
h. He was sent to preach repentance to Nineveh.
i. all-knowing
j. the capital city of Assyria

JUMP-STARTING THE LESSON

11. After spending the weekend with their friends, what did Jermaine and Donna do for each neighbor when they drove on their street (see the In Focus story)?

_____

12. According to the In Focus story, why are our neighborhoods our closest mission fields?

_____.

UNDERSTANDING THE LESSON

13. According to The People, Places, and Times, Jonah was the _____ of the _____ Prophets who prophesied during _____ reign.

14. As with other prophets, God called Jonah to preach _____ (see Background).

15. The people of Nineveh, who were Israel's enemies, were the _____ (Background).

16. List four of Nineveh's infractions and sins against God (Jonah 1:1, More Light on the Text).

a. _____

b. _____

c. _____

d. _____

17. When Jonah went to Tarshish, what four things was he trying to get away from (Jonah 1:1-3, In Depth, More Light on the Text)?

a. _____

b. _____

c. _____

d. _____

18. God had prepared the hearts of the Ninevites to receive both His message and to repent (Jonah 3:3, In Depth, More Light on the Text).

True   False

COMMITTING TO THE WORD

19. Why is there often a need for both prayer and fasting to break the cycle of sin for an individual, a peop a family, or a nation (Jonah 3:7, More Light on the Text)?

_____

_____

_____

b. Explanation:

_____

_____

_____

WALKING IN THE WORD

20. Share a time when you engaged in prayer and fasting to break the cycle of sin for an individual, a peopl a family, or our nation.

_____

_____

_____

_____

> "O LORD, was not this my saying, when I was yet in my country? Therefore I fled before unto Tarshish: for I knew that thou art a gracious God, and merciful, slow to anger, and of great kindness, and repentest thee of the evil" (Jonah 4:2).

A COMMUNITY TO REDEEM

JONAH 3:10—4:5

Use with Bible Study Guide 2.

WORDS AND PHRASES

Match the words, phrases, or names with the correct definitions.

1. ____ booth
2. ____ displeased
3. ____ gracious
4. ____ Jonah
5. ____ merciful
6. ____ repent
7. ____ shadow
8. ____ the Assyrians
9. ____ "the Feast of Tabernacles"
10. ___ works

a. deeds, labor, things done
b. to turn from sin and turn to God
c. symbolic of how life is transitory
d. a temporary shelter
e. the Israelites' enemies
f. grieved, furious, incensed
g. to be compassionate
h. the reluctant prophet
i. to show favor
j. a Jewish harvest festival

JUMP-STARTING THE LESSON

11. According to the In Focus story, God sends rain upon the _____ and the

_____.

12. According to the In Focus story, God loves _____.

UNDERSTANDING THE LESSON

13. Jonah's booth was the tent of his _____ _____ (The People, Places, and Times).

14. Jonah did not rejoice in his victory (when the Ninevites were spared from destruction), but instead wished for his own _____ (Background).

15 a. True repentance is more than simply apologizing for sins (Jonah 3:10, In Depth, More Light on the Text).   True   False

   b. Explain what "true repentance" is:

_____

_____

—

16. Why was Jonah angry with the Lord (Jonah 4:1–5, In Depth, More Light on the Text)?

_____

_____

_____

17. Jonah hoped that his prayer of frustration to God would result in Nineveh's _____ (Jonah 4:5, In Depth, More Light on the Text).

18. For whom is God's harsh judgment reserved (Jonah 4:5, In Depth, More Light on the Text)?

_____

_____

COMMITTING TO THE WORD

19. Fill in the blanks and memorize.

"O LORD, was not this my saying, when I was yet in my country? Therefore I _____ before unto

_____: for I knew that thou art a _____God, and _____,

_____ to anger, and of great _____, and repentest thee of the

_____" (Jonah 4:2).

WALKING IN THE WORD

20. Explain the following statement: "The Great Commission" is not just for our friends or people who have not hurt us or made us angry; we are to take the Gospel of Salvation to all of the world (Mark 16:15).

_____

_____

_____

_____

_____

_____

> *"And Ruth said, Intreat me not to leave thee, or to return from following after thee: for whither thou goest, I will go; and where thou lodgest, I will lodge: thy people shall be my people, and thy God my God"* (Ruth 1:16).

FAMILY AS COMMUNITY

RUTH 1:1–9, 14B, 16

Use with Bible Study Guide 3.

WORDS AND PHRASES

Match the words, phrases, or names with the correct definitions.

1. _____ Elimelech
2. _____ Ephrathah
3. _____ famine
4. _____ intreat
5. _____ Messiah
6. _____ Naomi
7. _____ Rahab
8. _____ Ruth
9. _____ sojourn
10. ___ the Moabites

a. to ask, to implore
b. descendants from Lot, Abraham's nephew
c. a man of Bethlehem; Naomi's husband
d. a former prostitute from Jericho; Boaz was her descendant
e. a time of extensive hunger
f. another name for Bethlehem
g. dwell in, dwell with
h. Ruth's mother-in-law
i. Jesus Christ
j. the great-grandmother of King David

JUMP-STARTING THE LESSON

11. According to the In Focus story, all families have problems; every family has some degree of dysfunction.
True   False

12. According to the In Focus story, the story of Ruth gives us a great example of what it means to be _____, especially in times of _____.

UNDERSTANDING THE LESSON

13. The book of Ruth is set against the terrible background of the _____ and foreign _____ during the period of the _____ (Background).

14. Because of a local famine, Elimelech (Naomi's husband) moved his family from _____ (the Promised Land) to _____ (a heathen land) (Ruth 1:1, In Depth, More Light on the Text).

15. Why didn't God want His chosen people (the Israelites) to intermarry with non-Israelites (Ruth 1:5–6, In Depth, More Light on the Text)?

_____

_____

16. After Naomi lost her husband and two sons, she was a _____ woman in spirit and needed to return home (the land of Judah) to be _____ (Ruth 1:5–6, In Depth, More Light on the Text).

17. Naomi acknowledged the fact that her two daughters-in-law had dealt kindly with her through many trials of their own. This showed that she was not a _____ woman, just thinking of her own _____ (Ruth 1:8, In Depth, More Light on the Text).

18. What was Naomi's parting blessing to Orpah and Ruth (Ruth 1:9, In Depth, More Light on the Text)?

_____

_____

_____

COMMITTING TO THE WORD

19. List four things that Ruth committed to doing with her mother-in-law that proved Ruth's faithfulness. Consider the weight of Ruth's commitment (Ruth 1:16, In Depth, More Light on the Text).

a. _____

b. _____

c. _____

d. _____

WALKING IN THE WORD

20. Share a time when you needed "spiritual" rest and God met your need.

_____

_____

_____

_____

_____

_____

_____

"And now, my daughter, fear not; I will do to thee all that thou requirest: for all the city of my people doth know that thou art a virtuous woman"
(Ruth 3:11)

ACCEPTANCE IN COMMUNITY

RUTH 2:5–12; 3:9–11

Use with Bible Study Guide 4.

WORDS AND PHRASES

Match the words, phrases, or names with the correct definitions.

1. ____ bath
2. ____ Boaz
3. ____ checed
4. ____ glean
5. ____ grace
6. ____ kinsman
7. ____ Mara
8. ____ Moab
9. ____ Naomi
10. ___ Obed

a. a name that means "bitter"
b. to pick up or gather
c. Her name means "pleasant"
d. Ruth's country; they were often at war with Israel
e. a Hebrew word for "daughter"
f. a wealthy farmer; a near relative to Naomi
g. a Hebraic concept that means "faithfulness or loyalty"
h. kindness, favor
i. Boaz and Ruth's son; the grandfather of King David
j. relative

JUMP-STARTING THE LESSON

11. Name four things that Mrs. Coulibaly did to help Jamilah feel like an accepted part of the class (see In Focus story).

a. _____

b. _____

c. _____

d. _____

12. According to the In Focus story, if we open our _____ and _____, we will see many people around us who do not seem like a part of the group.

UNDERSTANDING THE LESSON

13. Explain how Jesus Christ became our Kinsman-Redeemer (The People, Places, and Times).

_____

_____

_____

_____

14. Explain God's Law (the Levirate Law) concerning care for the poor (Background, Ruth 2:7, In Depth, M
Light on the Text).

_____

_____

_____

_____

15. Ruth's willingness to glean in the fields showed her _____ and _____ for her
mother-in-law, Naomi (Ruth 2:5; In Depth, More Light on the Text).

16. Boaz was a man of character (Ruth 2:5; In Depth, More Light on the Text).   True   False

17. Why did Boaz act kindly toward Ruth (Ruth 2:11, In Depth, More Light on the Text)?

_____

_____

18. Throughout the story of Ruth, there are overtones of God's _____ and _____
(Ruth 3:11, In Depth, More Light on the Text).

COMMITTING TO THE WORD
19. Why is the story of Ruth, Naomi, and Boaz so important (Ruth 3:9–11, In Depth, More Light on the Te)

_____

_____

_____

_____

WALKING IN THE WORD
20. List some important principles that you drew from the story of Ruth, Naomi, and Boaz:

_____

_____

_____

_____

_____

_____

_____

_____

_____

_____

_____

THE COMMUNITY FACES PAIN AND JOY

"A little while, and ye shall not see me: and again, a little while, and ye shall see me, because I go to the Father" (John 16:16).

JOHN 16:16–24; 20:11–16

Use with Bible Study Guide 5.

WORDS AND PHRASES

Match the words, phrases, or names with the correct definitions.

1. _____ angel
2. _____ anguish
3. _____ desire
4. _____ Holy Spirit
5. _____ Jesus
6. _____ joy
7. _____ lament
8. _____ Rabboni
9. _____ sepulchre
10. ___ travail

a. to bring forth, to bear, to produce
b. cheerfulness or delight
c. a tomb, a grave
d. means "My Great One" or "My Master"
e. messenger or one who is sent
f. to have in mind or to intend
g. the Third Person of the Trinity or Godhead
h. to bewail, to mourn
i. affliction, distress, oppression
j. the Risen Lord

JUMP-STARTING THE LESSON

11. According to the In Focus story, little Nathan's death illustrated that if we let it, _____ can sneak into our world and rob us of our _____.

12. According to the In Focus story, Jesus had to prepare His disciples and let them know that He would never _____ or _____ them; pain and _____ will be replaced by _____ and _____.

UNDERSTANDING THE LESSON

13. In the text, Jesus' death was only a few hours away (Background).   True   False

14. What three things did Jesus come into the world to do (Background)?
a. _____
b. _____
c. _____

15. We can have joy, regardless of life's circumstances, if we put our _____ in _____

and allow _____ to work out the _____ (John 16:16–20, In Depth).

16. Jesus knew that after His departure, His disciples would be responsible for helping the world to understand the _____ that was _____ in _____
(John 16:22, More Light on the Text).

17. Explain the meaning of the following: "Because of God's great love for His Son, the disciples would be able to ask anything of the Father in His name and it would be granted" (John 16:23, More Light on the Text).

_____

_____

_____

_____

18. Because of the way that they were dressed, Mary did not know that the two men at Jesus' tomb were angels (John 20:12, In Depth, More Light on the Text).   True   False

COMMITTING TO THE WORD

19. Fill in the blanks and memorize.

"A little while, and ye shall _____ _____ _____: and again, a little while, and ye shall _____ _____, because I go to the _____" (John 16:16).

WALKING IN THE WORD

20. Share a time when your joy was restored because you trusted in Jesus as your Source and allowed Him to work out the details of a pressing or painful situation in your life.

_____

_____

_____

_____

_____

_____

_____

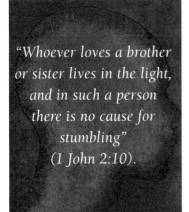

"Whoever loves a brother or sister lives in the light, and in such a person there is no cause for stumbling" (1 John 2:10).

LOVE WITHIN THE COMMUNITY

1 JOHN 2:9–11, 15–17

Use with Bible Study Guide 6.

WORDS AND PHRASES

Match the words, phrases, or names with the correct definitions.

1. ____ abiding
2. ____ antichrists
3. ____ "Christ's incarnation"
4. ____ Docetism
5. ____ "eternal life"
6. ____ "love for God"
7. ____ lust
8. ____ pride
9. ____ "the world"
10. ___ Zebedee

a. a system or order whose values are opposed to God
b. denotes a strong desire, craving, or longing
c. self-confidence, boasting, or arrogance
d. a fisherman and the father of John and James
e. Jesus became flesh or took on human flesh
f. everlasting
g. false teachers throughout the Asia Minor churches
h. staying in a place
i. it entails obedience to God's commands
j. denounced the saving work of Jesus Christ on the Cross

JUMP-STARTING THE LESSON

11. According to the In Focus story, in today's lesson, John calls for _____ to _____ _____ as _____ has _____ us.

12. We are _____ to _____ because God's _____ is _____ _____ in our _____ by the _____ _____ (In Focus story).

UNDERSTANDING THE LESSON

13. Early in the ministry Jesus called James and John "_____" (The People, Places, and Times).

14. List seven reasons why tradition has rendered the apostle John as the "beloved apostle" of Jesus (The People, Places, and Times).

a. _____
b. _____
c. _____
d. _____

e. _____

f. _____

g. _____

15. John insists that the person who _____ what is _____ and does what is _____ walks in the _____. In contrast, a person who does not _____ the _____ of _____ _____ and has broken fellowship with other _____ is _____ by _____ (1 John 2:9-11, In Depth).

16. John taught that a so-called Christian who habitually hates other believers is still in a _____ of _____ _____ and has not experienced _____ _____ (1 John 2:11, More Light on the Text).

17. The apostle John encouraged his readers to love others _____ as modeled by _____ (1 John 2:15, More Light on the Text).

18. Doing the will of God is a _____ that one is intentionally _____ to so that it becomes habitual (1 John 2:17, In Depth).

COMMITTING TO THE WORD

19. Fill in the blanks and memorize.

"No one can _____ _____ _____. Either he will _____ the _____ and _____ the _____, or he will be _____ to the one and _____ the other. You cannot serve both _____ and _____ [mammon]" (Matthew 6:24, NIV).

WALKING IN THE WORD

20. Define the "lust of the flesh," the "lust of the eyes," and "pride of life" and how you can avoid them (1 John 2:16, In Depth, More Light on the Text).

_____

_____

_____

_____

_____

_____

_____

"Jesus said unto him, Thou shalt love the Lord thy God with all thy heart, and with all thy soul, and with all thy mind" (Matthew 22:37).

CONNECTING IN COMMUNITY

MATTHEW 22:34–40

Use with Bible Study Guide 7.

WORDS AND PHRASES

Match the words, phrases, or names with the correct definitions.

1. ____ heart
2. ____ Master
3. ____ mind
4. ____ neighbor
5. ____ Pharisees
6. ____ Sadducees
7. ____ soul
8. ____ tempt
9. ____ the Torah
10. ___ the Sanhedrin

a. wealthier Jewish elite who ruled the temple
b. the Jewish Supreme Court
c. they developed and ran local Jewish synagogues
d. written law
e. to test one maliciously
f. anyone whom an individual comes in contact
g. the imagination, understanding
h. one who is fit to teach
i. that which animates us or moves us to action
j. refers to the thoughts and feelings

JUMP-STARTING THE LESSON

11. According to the In Focus story, when Jesus said that we should love the Lord God with all our minds, He was talking about our _____.

12. According to the In Focus story, God wants to be the _____ of our _____, our _____, and the _____ of the things we do.

UNDERSTANDING THE LESSON

13. The lawyer that asked Jesus the question, "Master, which is the greatest commandment in the law?", (Matthew 22:36) was himself an expert in the _____ (In Depth).

14. The Pharisees identified more than how many laws that formed the body of religious teaching for the nation of Israel (More Light on the Text)?
a. 200   b. 400   c. 600   d. 800   e. 1000

15. Jesus told the lawyer that the commandment "Thou shalt love the Lord thy God with all thy heart, and with all thy soul, and with all thy mind" sums up which four of the Ten Commandments found in Exodus 20:3–11, NLT (Matthew 22:37–38, In Depth, More Light on the Text)?

a. _____

b. _____

c. _____

d. _____

16. (a) What is the second greatest commandment (Matthew 22:39-40)?

_____

_____

(b) Name the six commandments that this great command sums up:

a. _____

b. _____

c. _____

d. _____

e. _____

f. _____

17. God placed before the Pharisees a new way of viewing the Law that valued _____ over _____ (Matthew 22:40, More Light on the Text).

18. Jesus sought to teach the religious leadership of His time that the way to truly show _____ for _____ was by _____ (Matthew 22:40, More Light on the Text).

COMMITTING TO THE WORD

19a. Memorize Matthew 22:37 and explain its meaning.

_____

_____

b. Explanation:

_____

_____

_____

WALKING IN THE WORD

20. Write a love letter to Jesus expressing what He means to you and thanking Him for His wonderful salvation

_____

_____

_____

"Go out quickly into the streets and lanes of the city, and bring in hither the poor, and the maimed, and the halt, and the blind" (Luke 14:21).

INCLUSION IN COMMUNITY

LUKE 14:15–24

Use with Bible Study Guide 8.

WORDS AND PHRASES

Match the words, phrases, or names with the correct definitions.

1. ____ blessed
2. ____ compel
3. ____ death
4. ____ God's grace
5. ____ halt
6. ____ prove
7. ____ taste
8. ____ "the bread of life"
9. ____ the kingdom of God
10. ___ Yahweh

a. God's rule, His realm, His reign
b. Jesus
c. the God of Abraham, Isaac and Jacob
d. fortunate, well off
e. to test
f. to necessitate, constrain
g. favor
h. limping, cripple, lame
i. experience
j. eternal separation from Holy God

JUMP-STARTING THE LESSON

11. According to the In Focus story, why did Kirk need to go to the mini-revival at his church?

_____

_____

12. According to the In Focus story, who will be a part of God's Kingdom?

_____

_____

UNDERSTANDING THE LESSON

13. List five attributes of humility discussed in The People, Places, and Times.

a. _____
b. _____
c. _____
d. _____
e. _____

14. Jesus and the Pharisees were allies (Luke 14:15, In Depth, More Light on the Text).

True   False

15. The Pharisees used _____ to rule as religious leaders (Luke 14:15, In Depth, More Light on the Text).

16. What is the personal invitation that God extends to all (Luke 14:15–24, In Depth, More Light on the Text)?

_____

_____

_____

_____

(John 3:16).

17. Believers are all the children of God by _____ in _____ (Luke 14:15-2 In Depth, More Light on the Text).

18. In essence, God sent His _____ and _____ _____ to a whole world of_____ _____ people (Luke 14:19–20, More Light on the Text).

COMMITTING TO THE WORD

19a. Memorize Luke 14:21.

b. Explain what Luke 14:21 means in relation to the "Great Commission" (Matthew 28:19–20).

_____

_____

_____

_____

WALKING IN THE WORD

20. Describe how you would carry out the Great Commission to "Go ye therefore, and teach all nations, baptizing them in the name of the Father, and of the Son, and of the Holy Ghost: Teaching them to observe all things whatsoever I have commanded you" (Matthew 28:19–20).

_____

_____

_____

_____

_____

"For this cause we also, since the day we heard it, do not cease to pray for you, and to desire that ye might be filled with the knowledge of his will in all wisdom and spiritual understanding" (Colossians 1:9).

A FAITHFUL COMMUNITY

COLOSSIANS 1:1–14

Use with Bible Study Guide 9.

WORDS AND PHRASES

Match the words, phrases, or names with the correct definitions.

1. ____ an apologist   a. quietness, rest
2. ____ Epaphras   b. choice, desire, volition
3. ____ epistle   c. been "ransomed in full"—believers' sin-penalty paid in full
4. ____ faith   d. forbearance, patience
5. ____ forgiveness   e. a defender of the Gospel
6. ____ hope   f. letter
7. ____ longsuffering   g. having full assurance that God will honor His promises
8. ____ peace   h. liberty, remission, pardon
9. ____ redemption   i. founded the church in Colosse
10. ___ will   j. expectation, confidence

JUMP-STARTING THE LESSON

11. According to the In Focus story, when God saved us He also welcomed us into _____ _____.

12. According to the In Focus story, what does recognizing our heavenly citizenship help us to see?

_____

_____

UNDERSTANDING THE LESSON

13. Who founded the church in Colosse (The People, Places, and Times)?

a. Paul   b. Peter   c. Silus   d. Epaphras

14. The church met in _____ home (The People, Places, and Times).

15. What did the Gospel of Jesus Christ tell the Colossians of (Colossians 1:3–8, In Depth, More Light on the Text)?

_____

_____

16a. The heresy that had crept into the Colossian church was similar to _____.

b. Name one thing that these heretics believed and taught (Colossians 1:1, In Depth, More Light on the Text).

_____

_____

17. What did hearing the truth of the Gospel do for the Colossians (Colossians 1:6, In Depth, More Light on the Text)?

_____

_____

18. Paul and his companions prayed that whatever the Colossians' circumstances, they would be _____ by the mighty power of God with _____, _____ or _____, and with the _____ that comes from God (Colossians 1:11, More Light on the Text).

COMMITTING TO THE WORD

19a. Memorize Colossians 1:12–14.

b. Explain the meaning of Colossians 1:12–14.

_____

_____

_____

_____

WALKING IN THE WORD

20. What does it mean to you to have a portion in the inheritance that God has promised all believers?

_____

_____

_____

_____

_____

_____

_____

"Beware lest any man spoil you through philosophy and vain deceit, after the tradition of men, after the rudiments of the world, and not after Christ" (Colossians 2:8).

AN ESTABLISHED COMMUNITY

COLOSSIANS 2:1–10

Use with Bible Study Guide 10.

WORDS AND PHRASES

Match the words, phrases, or names with the correct definitions.

1. _____ beguile
2. _____ conflict
3. _____ Godhead
4. _____ knowledge
5. _____ mystery
6. _____ rooted
7. _____ take captive
8. _____ the "God-man"
9. _____ vain
10. _____ walk

a. a hidden or secret thing
b. brings forth nothing of value
c. powerfully enslave
d. Jesus Christ
e. the daily life and habits of the believer
f. moral wisdom, such as seen in right living
g. deceive, delude
h. rendered firm, established
i. agony
j. Supreme Deity, the essential being of God, the Supreme Being

JUMP-STARTING THE LESSON

11. According to the In Focus story, what are two problems that personal ideologies and New Age thinking can cause in a church body?

a. _____

b. _____

12. According to the In Focus story, to remain anchored in the Gospel truth, believers need to:

a. _____

b. _____

UNDERSTANDING THE LESSON

13. The Gnostics ignored or diminished the significance of the historic facts of the _____, _____, and _____ of Jesus Christ (The People, Places, and Times).

14. The letters of Paul and the other apostles were circulated throughout all churches to provide system-wide _____ and _____ (Colossians 2:1–3, In Depth).

15. What is "God's mystery" that the apostle Paul spoke of in Colossians 2:2 (In Depth, More Light on the Text)?

_____

_____

_____

_____

16. In warning against strange or false teachings, the apostle Paul told the church at Colosse to do what three things (Colossians 2:4–8, In Depth, More Light on the Text)?

a. _____

_____

b. _____

_____

c. _____

_____

17. The false teachers were teaching the Colossians a perilous mix of _____, _____ and _____ (Colossians 2:4, More Light on the Text).

18. When telling the Colossians to "walk ye in him [Christ]," the apostle spoke of their walking or living according to the true doctrine passed down from the _____ to the _____ (Colossians 2:6, More Light on the Text).

COMMITTING TO THE WORD

19. Explain what it means to be "Rooted and built up in him [Christ], and established in the faith"

(Colossians 2:7, In Depth, More Light on the Text).

Explanation:

a. "rooted": _____

_____

b. "built up in Christ": _____

_____

c. "established": _____

WALKING IN THE WORD

20. Explain how you are "complete" in Christ.

_____

_____

_____

"Put on therefore, as the elect of God, holy and beloved, bowels of mercies, kindness, humbleness of mind, meekness, longsuffering" (Colossians 3:12).

A CHOSEN COMMUNITY

COLOSSIANS 3:12–17

Use with Bible Study Guide 11.

WORDS AND PHRASES

Match the words, phrases, or names with the correct definitions.

1. ____ elect
2. ____ forbearing
3. ____ holy
4. ____ humility
5. ____ mercy
6. ____ "new man"
7. ____ "old man"
8. ____ patient
9. ____ the Holy Spirit
10. ___ "to put off"

a. thinking of others as better than ourselves
b. compassion
c. He gives believers power to obey and be Christlike
d. to get rid of
e. forgiving
f. set apart by God
g. for God to choose
h. coming to life after the pattern of Christ
i. one perishing after the pattern of Adam
j. longsuffering

JUMP-STARTING THE LESSON

11. According to the In Focus story, Evelyn felt that her adopted parents were not perfect, but they modeled in their lives the _____ of _____ _____.

12. According to the In Focus story, because we as believers are also chosen by Christ, there are expectations for us as His children.   True   False

UNDERSTANDING THE LESSON

13. According to The People, Places, and Times, what does "election" mean?

_____

_____

14. "Election" means that believers are proud to be chosen by God (The People, Places, and Times).
True   False

15. According to the apostle Paul, what things should we get rid of in our lives (Background)?

_____

_____

16. List at least nine virtues that the apostle Paul told the holy-chosen community of God to clothe themselv in (Colossians 3:12–15, In Depth, More Light on the Text).

a. _____   b. _____

c. _____   d. _____

e. _____   f. _____

g. _____   h. _____

i. _____

17. Explain why the apostle Paul said that we should forgive others based on what Christ has done for us (Colossians 3:13, In Depth, More Light on the Text).

_____

_____

_____

18. Explain what the apostle Paul meant by "And let the peace of God rule in your hearts" (Colossians 3:15, In Depth, More Light on the Text).

_____

_____

_____

COMMITTING TO THE WORD

19. Share how you felt to be forgiven by a loved one or coworker and then by God.

_____

_____

_____

_____

WALKING IN THE WORD

20. What does it mean to you to be "one with Christ"?

_____

_____

_____

_____

_____

_____

_____

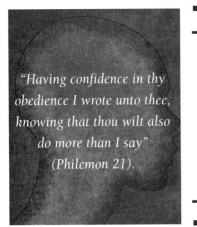

"Having confidence in thy obedience I wrote unto thee, knowing that thou wilt also do more than I say" (Philemon 21).

AT HOME IN THE COMMUNITY

PHILEMON 8–18

Use with Bible Study Guide 12.

WORDS AND PHRASES

Match the words, phrases, or names with the correct definitions.

1. ____ agape love
2. ____ appeal
3. ____ beseech
4. ____ bold
5. ____ Onesimus
6. ____ partner
7. ____ Philemon
8. ____ profitable
9. ____ Timothy
10. ___ unprofitable

a. a wealthy landowner, a slave owner
b. Paul's partner in ministry
c. means "unconditional"
d. detrimental
e. to implore, to call for, to exhort
f. invite, invoke, entreat
g. frankness, bluntness, outspokenness
h. an associate, companion, partaker
i. a runaway slave
j. useful

JUMP-STARTING THE LESSON

11. As raised in the In Focus story, what do you think are some of the most effective ways to stand up for someone or an important issue?

a. _____

b. _____

c. _____

12. According to the In Focus story, the apostle Paul was in _____ for preaching the _____ _____, but he still stands up for _____, a runaway slave.

UNDERSTANDING THE LESSON

13. Why was there ambiguity in the slave system of the Roman Empire (The People, Places, and Times)?

_____

_____

14. In the Roman Empire, a returned slave was usually branded with the letter _____ on his forehead, which stood for _____ and meant "runaway" (The People, Places, and Times).

15. When Paul wrote the letter to Philemon, he was under _____ (Introduction, More Light on the Text).

16. Paul's appeal to Philemon on behalf of Onesimus was based on what four Christian actions (Philemon 8–18, In Depth, More Light on the Text)?

a. _____   b. _____
c. _____   d. _____

17. Paul asked Philemon to do what two things in regard to Onesimus (Philemon 10, More Light on the Text)?

a. _____
b. _____

18. The apostle Paul did not _____ or _____ slavery, but worked instead to _____ like the one between Philemon and Onesimus (Philemon 12, In Depth, More Light on the Text).

COMMITTING TO THE WORD

19. Explain what the following statements mean: "Even in our own society, we find that we cannot legislate a change of heart. Only God can change and does change hearts."

_____
_____
_____
_____

WALKING IN THE WORD

20. As a child of God, what can you do to help bring about reconciliation in your family, the workplace, or even among races?

_____
_____
_____
_____
_____
_____
_____
_____

"And of some have compassion, making a difference: And others save with fear, pulling them out of the fire; hating even the garment spotted by the flesh" (Jude 1:22-23).

AT RISK IN THE COMMUNITY

JUDE 1:3–7, 19–21, 24–25

Use with Bible Study Guide 13.

WORDS AND PHRASES

Match the words, phrases, or names with the correct definitions.

1. _____ apostates
2. _____ fornication
3. _____ grace
4. _____ heretics
5. _____ holy
6. _____ Jude
7. _____ licentiousness
8. _____ power
9. _____ vengeance
10. ___ wrath

a. saints, sacred, pure, blameless
b. Jesus' half-brother
c. moral perversion
d. traitors
e. false teachers
f. fury, anger
g. to suffer punishment
h. an unbridled pursuit and embrace of sexual fulfillment
i. God's unmerited (undeserving) favor
j. force, competency, authority, liberty, strength

JUMP-STARTING THE LESSON

11. According to the In Focus story, of what two things did Jude warn his readers?

a. _____
b. _____

12. As raised in the In Focus story, what can we do as believers to help those in our communities to turn to Jesus and righteous living?

a. _____
b. _____
c. _____

UNDERSTANDING THE LESSON

13. In regard to Jude's instructions, explain the meaning of "antinomianism" (Background).

_____
_____

14. Jude urged the believers to defend the faith that God has entrusted to His church (Jude 3–7, In Depth, More Light on the Text).
True   False

15. What were two aspects of the heresy that Jude preached about that can be found in various beliefs of today (Jude 3–7, In Depth, More Light on the Text)?

a. _____

_____

b. _____

_____

16. List three final descriptions of the heretics that Jude discussed (Jude 19, More Light on the Text).

a. _____

_____

b._____

c._____

17. Explain the following statement: "Leaders are to be examples (walking and living letters or epistles) of righteousness for those they are leading" (Jude 19, More Light on the Text).

_____

_____

_____

18. Why did Jude urge his readers to keep on praying in the Holy Spirit (Jude 20, In Depth, More Light on the Text)?

_____

_____

_____

COMMITTING TO THE WORD

19. Explain why God is the only One who can keep believers from stumbling and falling prey to false teachers or doctrines (Jude 24, In Depth, More Light on the Text).

_____

_____

WALKING IN THE WORD

20. Explain what Jesus in the role of your Deliverer means to you.

_____

_____

_____

"And ye became followers of us, and of the Lord, having received the word in much affliction, with joy of the Holy Ghost" (1 Thessalonians 1:6).

VISIBLE TO GOD

1 THESSALONIANS 1

Use with Bible Study Guide 1.

WORDS AND PHRASES

Match the words, phrases, or names with the correct definitions.

1. ____ election
2. ____ faith
3. ____ "living epistles"
4. ____ omnipotent
5. ____ patience
6. ____ Paul
7. ____ Silas
8. ____ Thessalonica
9. ____ Timothy
10. ___ wrath

a. anger, indignation, punishment
b. He and Paul brought the message of salvation to the Thessalonians.
c. the capital of the Roman province of Macedonia
d. He became a believer during Paul's first missionary journey.
e. assurance, belief, moral conviction
f. divine selection, picking out, choosing
g. an apostle who helped shape the history of Christianity
h. endurance, constancy, steadfastness
i. all-powerful
j. doers of God's Word

JUMP-STARTING THE LESSON

11. In the In Focus story, why did Clara's family members persecute her?

_____

_____

12. According to the In Focus story, what did Clara do when her family members persecuted her?

_____

_____

UNDERSTANDING THE LESSON

13. According to The People, Places, and Times, with what were the new Christians in Thessalonica struggling? _____

14. According to the Background, there were misunderstandings concerning what?

_____

_____

15. Give four reasons that Paul wrote his letter to believers at Thessalonica (see Background).

a. _____

b. _____

c. _____

d. _____

16. The believers at Thessalonica had been faithful in (1 Thessalonians 1:2–3, In Depth):

a. _____

b. _____

c. _____

17. The message of salvation brought the church at Thessalonica both great joy and great persecution (1 Thessalonians 1:4–7, In Depth).   True   False

18. What was the testimony of the church at Thessalonica (1 Thessalonians 1:9, More Light on the Text)?

a. _____

b. _____

c. _____

d. _____

COMMITTING TO THE WORD

19. According to Revelation 21:1–4, what do you and all believers have to look forward to at Jesus' second coming (More Light on the Text)? "No more _____, or _____, or _____, or _____."

WALKING IN THE WORD

20. Do you believe in the second coming of Jesus Christ? Why? Why not? What did Jesus do for you on His first coming?

_____

_____

_____

_____

"But as we were allowed of God to be put in trust with the gospel, even so we speak; not as pleasing men, but God, which trieth our hearts" (1 Thessalonians 2:4).

PLEASING TO GOD

1 THESSALONIANS 2:1–12

Use with Bible Study Guide 2.

WORDS AND PHRASES

Match the words, phrases, or names with the correct definitions.

1. _____ cherish
2. _____ deceit
3. _____ exhortation
4. _____ flattery
5. _____ glory
6. _____ holy
7. _____ Christ
8. _____ travail
9. _____ uncleanness
10. ___ vain

a. fruitless; having no purpose or effect
b. an unhindered manifestation of God's presence in which believers will share
c. moral lewdness
d. to foster, to nourish
e. the trouble and pain of arduous work
f. to lie or cheat to worm one's way into peoples' hearts
g. using fair words to gain one's own selfish end
h. teaching, encouragement, consolation, comfort
i. set apart from sin
j. means "anointed one"

JUMP-STARTING THE LESSON

11. What were the two topics discussed at the conference that Pastor Thomas and the church's leadership team attended (see the In Focus story)?

a. _____

b. _____

12. According to the In Focus story, all believers should have an earnest _____ to please _____.

UNDERSTANDING THE LESSON

13. How many cities did Paul's second missionary trip encompass (Background)?

a. 5   b. 7   c. 10   d. 12   e. 15

14. In Paul's letter to the believers at Thessalonica, Paul applauded the Thessalonians for their commitment to _____ and spread the _____, especially in the face of _____ (1 Thessalonians 2:1–2, In Depth).

15. List five topics that the apostle Paul specifically addressed in his letter to the church at Thessalonica (1 Thessalonians 2:3–9, In Depth).

a. _____   b. _____

c. _____   d. _____

e. _____

16. Because Paul and his team bore good fruit in the lives of others, they reaped God's hand upon their ministries (1 Thessalonians 2:3-9, In Depth).   True   False

17. In his letter, Paul made it clear that pleasing God coincides with pleasing humanity (1 Thessalonians 2:1 12, In Depth).   True   False

18. According to the apostle Paul, above all else, _____ is a key element to pleasing God (1 Thessalonians 2:10–12, In Depth).

COMMITTING TO THE WORD

19. The apostle Paul taught that "pure motives produce pure service" (1 Thessalonians 2:3-9, In Depth). Wh does that mean to you in your walk with the Lord?

_____

_____

_____

_____

_____

WALKING IN THE WORD

20. Explain Jesus' first coming and relate it to His second.

_____

_____

_____

_____

_____

_____

_____

_____

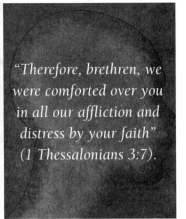

"Therefore, brethren, we were comforted over you in all our affliction and distress by your faith" (1 Thessalonians 3:7).

SUSTAINED THROUGH ENCOURAGEMENT

1 THESSALONIANS 3

Use with Bible Study Guide 3.

WORDS AND PHRASES

1. ____ abound
2. ____ affliction
3. ____ blameless
4. ____ comfort
5. ____ faith
6. ____ holy
7. ____ joy
8. ____ Septuagint
9. ____ stand
10. ___ the tempter

a. the Greek translation of the Old Testament
b. a call for continued steadfastness or perseverance
c. emotional or physical distress
d. Satan
e. to encourage, strengthen
f. to overflow
g. something or someone judged acceptable before God
h. trust in God
i. to be glad
j. a state or condition of that which was sanctified or consecrated as God's special possession

JUMP-STARTING THE LESSON

11. According to the In Focus story, how did the Ellises and Taylors support each other in their struggles dealing with their autistic children?

_____

12. According to the In Focus story, why did the apostle Paul send Timothy to the Thessalonians?

_____.

UNDERSTANDING THE LESSON

13. Where was Paul when he wrote his letter to the Thessalonians (Background)?

a. Berea   b. Athens   c. Thessalonica   d. Corinth

14. Why was Paul's journey to Thessalonica cut short (1 Thessalonians 3:1–5, In Depth)?

_____
_____

15. What was Timothy's sole purpose in visiting the believers at Thessalonica (1 Thessalonians 3:1–5, In Depth)?

_____

_____

16. According to the apostle Paul, Satan's job is "to

_____, _____, and _____

" (1 Thessalonians 3:1–5, In Depth).

17. What three petitions did Paul pray in regards to the Thessalonian believers (1 Thessalonians 3:11–13, In Depth, More Light on the Text)?

a. _____

b. _____

c. _____

18. Why did Paul desire that the church at Thessalonica might "abound" in love (1 Thessalonians 3:12–13, Depth, More Light on the Text)?

_____

_____

COMMITTING TO THE WORD

19. The apostle Paul instructed the believers at Thessalonica that afflictions are part of a normal Christian li (1 Thessalonians 3:3, In Depth, More Light on the Text). How do you view afflictions in your walk (everyda living) with God?

_____

_____

_____

WALKING IN THE WORD

20. Paul's words to the believers at Thessalonica connoted a relationship to God that also had ethical implic tions: God's saints, or holy ones, are those belonging and are dedicated to Him and His service. Explain wha the foregoing statements mean to you.

_____

_____

_____

"Furthermore then we beseech you, brethren, and exhort you by the Lord Jesus, that as ye have received of us how ye ought to walk and to please God, so ye would abound more and more" (1 Thessalonians 4:1).

DEMONSTRATED IN ACTION

1 THESSALONIANS 4:1–12

Use with Bible Study Guide 4.

WORDS AND PHRASES

Match the words, phrases, or names with the correct definitions.

1. ____ beseech
2. ____ exhort
3. ____ fornication
4. ____ "philadelphia"
5. ____ sanctification
6. ____ "the Christian walk"
7. ____ "the Holy Spirit"
8. ____ "the Saviour"
9. ____ vessel
10. ___ "worthily"

a. the spiritual and moral direction of a person's life; one's lifestyle
b. decently
c. the Agent of true holiness
d. holiness; consecration or separation from the world
e. to ask
f. sexual immorality
g. to urge
h. the human body
i. means "brotherly love"
j. the One who will act in judgment against those who are sinners in the church

JUMP-STARTING THE LESSON

11. According to the In Focus story, God has commanded us to live _____ and _____ lives and not to mix with the _____ of this world.

12. According to the In Focus story, Paul admonished the Thessalonians to live holy lives that are _____ to God.

UNDERSTANDING THE LESSON

13. The apostle Paul prayed that believers would be sanctified _____ and _____ (see Background).

14. Sanctification deals with what two areas of our lives (1 Thessalonians 4:1–8, In Depth)?
a. _____
b. _____

15. Compare and contrast the attributes of "positional sanctification" and "practical sanctification" (1 Thessalonians 4:1-8, In Depth).

a. _____

b. _____

c. _____

16. The ultimate purpose of living as a Christian is not to please ourselves, but to please God (1 Thessalonians 4:1, More Light on the Text).   True   False

17. The apostle Paul taught that because believers are under grace (God's favor) and not under the Law, we are not obligated to maintain much higher standards than those who do not have a relationship with God (1 Thessalonians 4:5, In Depth, More Light on the Text).   True   False

18. Paul taught that the reason for purity in believers' lives lies in the purpose of God's call that comes to people who enter into His kingdom (1 Thessalonians 4:7, More Light on the Text).   True   False

COMMITTING TO THE WORD

19. The ethical and spiritual demand for sanctification that was made by Paul rests, not in his teaching or the teaching of any person in particular, but in the nature and will of God (1 Thessalonians 4:8, More Light on the Text). Explain what this statement means to you in your walk (everyday living) with God.

_____

_____

_____

_____

_____

_____

WALKING IN THE WORD

20. Explain why believers should "walk honestly toward them that are without" or "walk worthily toward those outside of the church" (1 Thessalonians 4:12, In Depth, More Light on the Text). What does this mean in your lifestyle?

_____

_____

_____

_____

"For God hath not appointed us to wrath, but to obtain salvation by our Lord Jesus Christ" (1 Thessalonians 5:9).

GOD'S COSMIC PLAN

1 THESSALONIANS 5:1–11

Use with Bible Study Guide 5.

WORDS AND PHRASES

Match the words, phrases, or names with the correct definitions.

1. ____ "being awake"
2. ____ "children of the day"
3. ____ "God's Good News"
4. ____ predestination
5. ____ "saddle up"
6. ____ season
7. ____ "the breastplate"
8. ____ "the day of the Lord"
9. ____ "the dead"
10. ___ watch

a. an appointed time
b. "those who fall asleep"
c. a time of Christ's second coming
d. It guards a person's heart.
e. believers
f. being sober
g. to be alert
h. two parallel destinies for humankind
i. God's message of salvation
j. "put on our spiritual armor"

JUMP-STARTING THE LESSON

11. In the In Focus story, what did the policeman tell Brandon?

_____

_____

12. According to the In Focus story, the apostle Paul explained to the Thessalonians that "the day of the Lord" would come as a _____ in the _____.

UNDERSTANDING THE LESSON

13. In describing Christ's return to Earth, the apostle Paul indicated that Christ will descend from the _____ with a _____ (see Background).

14. Only _____ and the _____ know the time of Christ's return (1 Thessalonians 5:1–3, In Depth).

15. How does the apostle Paul describe the posture of "the children of the day" until Jesus' second coming (1 Thessalonians 5:4–6, In Depth)? Believers are:

a. _____

b. _____

c. _____

d. _____

16. How did the Thessalonians become a part of this "life-giving" day—"the day of the Lord" (1 Thessalonians 5:5, More Light on the Text)?

_____

_____

17. To those "in the night"—those sleeping; unbelievers—Christ's second coming will be an unpleasant surprise (1 Thessalonians 5:7, More Light on the Text).
True   False

18. How is God's righteousness worked out through the church (1 Thessalonians 5:8, More Light on the Text)? It is worked out in _____ and _____.

COMMITTING TO THE WORD

19. God has control over history and salvation. Explain what the foregoing statement means to believers and unbelievers (1 Thessalonians 5:9, More Light on the Text).

_____

_____

_____

_____

_____

_____

_____

WALKING IN THE WORD

20. Christ's "atoning" work on the Cross is what actually delivers salvation to those who are His. What does the foregoing statement mean to you?

_____

_____

_____

_____

> "Wherefore also we pray always for you, that our God would count you worthy of this calling, and fulfill all the good pleasure of his goodness, and the work of faith with power"
> (2 Thessalonians 1:11).

GLORY TO CHRIST

2 THESSALONIANS 1:3–12

Use with Bible Study Guide 6.

WORDS AND PHRASES

Match the words or names with the correct definitions.

1. ____ "being qualified"
2. ____ bound
3. ____ charity
4. ____ merit
5. ____ omnipresent
6. ____ omniscient
7. ____ recompense
8. ____ Stephen
9. ____ the Holy Spirit
10. ___ worthy

a. to render, to repay, to requite (good or evil)
b. His death served as a catalyst to take the Gospel worldwide.
c. owed, under obligation
d. He empowers us to live for Christ.
e. being made fit for God's kingdom
f. deemed entitled to
g. to obtain a reward by works
h. all-knowing
i. love, affection, or benevolence
j. all-present

JUMP-STARTING THE LESSON

11. What did Marilyn mean when she asked her Sunday School teacher to "please pray our strength in the Lord" (see the In Focus story)?

_____

_____

12. According to the In Focus story, being a Christian exempts us from life's many problems.

    True   False

UNDERSTANDING THE LESSON

13. Who founded the church at Thessalonica on Paul's second missionary journey (see Background)?

_____

14. Explain the following statement: "It is extremely important to trust God's timing and His faithfulness in our times of trouble" (2 Thessalonians 1:3–10, In Depth).

_____

_____

15. What two petitions did other believers make for the Thessalonians in their intercessory prayers (2 Thessalonians 1:11–12, In Depth)?

a. _____

b. _____

16. Explain the following statement: "God's justification of believers" (2 Thessalonians 1:3, More Light on the Text).

_____

_____

17. What two qualities did Paul find in the believers at Thessalonica that encouraged him and the other churches (2 Thessalonians 1:4, More Light on the Text)? He found _____ and _____

18. Explain the following statement: "God is a consuming fire" (2 Thessalonians 1:8, More Light on the Te)

_____

_____

COMMITTING TO THE WORD

19. What is an element of the misery of hell (2 Thessalonians 1:9, More Light on the Text)?

_____

_____

_____

WALKING IN THE WORD

20. Share a time when you had to trust God's timing and faithfulness in your season of trouble.

_____

_____

_____

_____

_____

_____

_____

_____

_____

_____

_____

"Therefore, brethren, stand fast, and hold the traditions which ye have been taught, whether by word, or our epistle"
(2 Thessalonians 2:15).

CHOSEN AND CALLED

2 THESSALONIANS 2:13–17

Use with Bible Study Guide 7.

WORDS AND PHRASES

Match the words or names with the correct definitions.

1. ____ called
2. ____ consolation
3. ____ everlasting
4. ____ inerrant
5. ____ grace
6. ____ heart
7. ____ hold
8. ____ hope
9. ____ persevere
10. ___ sanctification

a. God's special favor, reward
b. the center and seat of spiritual life
c. to stand fast in one's calling, in the faith
d. encouragement, comfort, solace
e. eternal, forever, without beginning and end
f. invited, named by name
g. without error
h. the state of purity, holiness
i. use strength, be master of
j. joyful and confident expectation

JUMP-STARTING THE LESSON

11. How did the following Scripture help John and Mary in their decision on whether to leave or remain at their church: "They that are whole need not a physician: but they that are sick. I came not to call the righteous, but sinners to repentance" (Luke 5:30–32, see the In Focus story)?

_____

_____

_____

12. According to the In Focus story, God is calling for commitment to _____ agenda—saving _____ _____, helping to _____ _____ _____.

UNDERSTANDING THE LESSON

13. According to The People, Places, and Times, genuine faith and perseverance are not the result of having faith in _____, but _____ in _____.

14. What are two blessings that come from perseverance and faith in Almighty God (see The People, Places, and Times)?

a. _____
b. _____

15. Believers' salvation is all about God and His work of building His kingdom that will reign forever and ever (2 Thessalonians 2:13–14, In Depth).　　　True　　　False

16. Why is false teaching or doctrine a threat to the church (2 Thessalonians 2:15–17, In Depth)?

_____

_____

_____

_____

17. The apostle Paul urged the believers at Thessalonica to _____ and hold on to the _____ _____ that they had been taught from the beginning of their faith (2 Thessalonians 2:15–17, In Depth, More Light on the Text).

18. Explain what it means to be "established in the ways of God" (2 Thessalonians 2:17, In Depth, More Li on the Text).

_____

_____

COMMITTING TO THE WORD

19. How did God show His unconditional love for you (2 Thessalonians 1:16, More Light on the Text)?

_____

_____

WALKING IN THE WORD

20. Will you one day reign with Christ in the New Jerusalem forever and ever? What does this reign mean to you

_____

_____

_____

_____

_____

_____

_____

_____

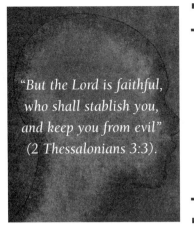

"But the Lord is faithful, who shall stablish you, and keep you from evil" (2 Thessalonians 3:3).

GOD'S OWN FAITHFULNESS

2 THESSALONIANS 3:1–15

Use with Bible Study Guide 8.

WORDS AND PHRASES

Match the words or names with the correct definitions.

1. ____ busybodies
2. ____ confidence
3. ____ direct
4. ____ "fruitful witness"
5. ____ preserve
6. ____ slothful
7. ____ "stablish"
8. ____ "the day of the Lord"
9. ____ undergird
10. ___ unreasonable

a. the second coming of Christ
b. improper, wicked, unrighteous, harmful
c. lazy
d. to build one's hope on the firm foundation (God)
e. to pray believers through their trials
f. to have belief in, faith in, trust in
g. to guide, remove hindrances
h. positive presence that brings others to Christ
i. persons nosing into others' business
j. to keep

JUMP-STARTING THE LESSON

11. Why did Robert feel convicted and begin to reevaluate his commitment as the Community Health Coordinator at a local health clinic (see the In Focus story)?

_____

_____

12. Using the In Focus story, list three challenges that can cause us to become "weary in well doing."

a. _____
b. _____
c. _____

UNDERSTANDING THE LESSON

13. _____ is essential in any spiritual battle (2 Thessalonians 3:1–5, In Depth).

14. Why is it imperative that believers put on the whole armor of God and encourage one another to stand firm in the faith (2 Thessalonians 3:1–5, In Depth)?

_____

_____

15. The apostle Paul advised the Thessalonians to pray so "that the word of the Lord may have free course, and be glorified" (2 Thessalonians 3:1, In Depth, More Light on the Text). List four hindrances to the spread of the Word of God.

a. _____

b. _____

c. _____

d. _____

16. List some of the ways that God establishes us and keeps us from evil (2 Thessalonians 3:2, More Light on the Text).

a. _____

b. _____

c. _____

d. _____

17. The apostle Paul prayed that through the _____ _____, the Thessalonians' hearts would be brought—guided into the _____ of _____ (2 Thessalonians 3:5, In Depth, More Light on the Text).

18. Why did Paul command the Thessalonians to withdraw for a time from every brother that walked disorderly (2 Thessalonians 3:6, In Depth, More Light on the Text)?

_____

_____

_____

COMMITTING TO THE WORD

19. As was the case with apostle Paul, can your life be used as an example of how to live the Christian life (2 Thessalonians 3:7, More Light on the Text)? Why? Why not?

_____

_____

_____

WALKING IN THE WORD

20. How has a fellow believer encouraged you or another saint in a lingering spiritual battle?

_____

_____

_____

_____

> *"Only let your conversation be as it becometh the gospel of Christ: that whether I come and see you, or else be absent, I may hear of your affairs, that ye stand fast in one spirit, with one mind striving together for the faith of the gospel"*
> *(Philippians 1:27).*

SHARING GOD'S GRACE

PHILIPPIANS 1:18B-29

Use with Bible Study Guide 9.

WORDS AND PHRASES

Match the words or names with the correct definitions.

1. _____ conversation
2. _____ epistle
3. _____ flesh
4. _____ furtherance
5. _____ hope
6. _____ magnify
7. _____ perdition
8. _____ Spirit
9. _____ "take pride"
10. ___ token

a. to enlarge, to declare to be great
b. eternal, spiritual damnation
c. proof
d. boast, glory in, rejoice
e. advancing, moving forward
f. refers to the human body
g. to expect with great confidence and faith
h. behavior or manner of life
i. letter
j. the third Person of the Trinity

JUMP-STARTING THE LESSON

11. How does the In Focus story define "what it means to be alive"?

_____

_____

12. According to the In Focus story, believers' hope is built on _____ and His

_____.

UNDERSTANDING THE LESSON

13. According to the Background, Paul's epistle to the Philippians is another of his letters from

_____.

14. The main theme in this short letter is _____ and _____(see Background).

15. Why was apostle Paul rejoicing in his letter to the Philippians (Philippians 1:18b–20, In Depth, More Light on the Text)?

_____

_____

16. How did Paul view "death" and "life" (Philippians 1:21–24, In Depth, More Light on the Text)?

_____

_____

17. According to apostle Paul, what does it mean to live as "citizens of heaven" (Philippians 1:27–29, In Depth, More Light on the Text)?

a. _____

b. _____

c. _____

d. _____

18. Paul considered suffering for Christ to be a _____ (Philippians 1:27–29, In Depth, More Lig on the Text).

COMMITTING TO THE WORD

19. Share a time in your life when it was a privilege to suffer for Christ.

_____

_____

_____

_____

WALKING IN THE WORD

20. As the apostle Paul was, are you so in love with the Lord that you would far rather be with Him? Why? Why not?

_____

_____

_____

_____

_____

_____

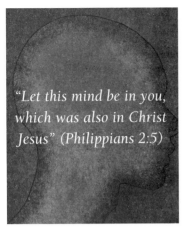

"Let this mind be in you, which was also in Christ Jesus" (Philippians 2:5)

GIVING OF ONESELF

PHILIPPIANS 2:1–13

Use with Bible Study Guide 10.

WORDS AND PHRASES

Match the words or names with the correct definitions.

1. ____ bowels
2. ____ "bowels and mercies"
3. ____ confess
4. ____ "fear and trembling"
5. ____ humility
6. ____ likeminded
7. ____ mindset
8. ____ sovereignty
9. ____ the Kenosis
10. ___ work out

a. to be earnestly concerned about the same things
b. attitude
c. have an awe and reverence to God for saving you
d. in control and never out of control
e. performing, accomplishing, or achieving
f. heart
g. acknowledge
h. love and compassion
i. to bring low
j. Jesus emptied Himself when He became fully man (He became a servant).

JUMP-STARTING THE LESSON

11. According to the In Focus story, following Jesus' example means giving of _____.

12. According to the In Focus story, Jesus took _____ upon Himself and then _____ on the _____.

UNDERSTANDING THE LESSON

13. According to The People, Places, and Times, "the Kenosis" speaks of Christ's:
a. _____ b. _____
c. _____ d. _____
e. _____ f. _____

14. When Jesus became fully man, He emptied Himself of His divine attributes (see The People, Places, and Times).   True   False

15. What were the apostle Paul's two appeals with which he began and ended the letter to the Philippians (Philippians 2:1–4, In Depth, More Light on the Text)?

a. _____

b. _____

16. Believers' relationships with people, even people we do not like or disagree with sharply, is determined by our relationship to our _____, _____ _____ (Philippians 2:1-4, In Depth).

17. Paul wanted the Philippians to develop the same _____, _____, _____, and _____ (Philippians 2:1–4, In Depth, More Light on the Text).

18. Name three attributes of the believer's sanctification (Philippians 2:12–13, More Light on the Text). Sanctification is:

a. _____

b. _____

c. _____

COMMITTING TO THE WORD

19. How do you "work out" your salvation with "fear and trembling" (Philippians 2:12-13, In Depth, More Light on the Text)?

_____

_____

_____

_____

WALKING IN THE WORD

20. What does it mean to you that "when Jesus became man, He *never* stopped being God"?

_____

_____

_____

_____

_____

_____

_____

_____

_____

> "Brethren, I count not myself to have apprehended: but this one thing I do, forgetting those things which are behind, and reaching forth unto those things which are before, I press toward the mark for the prize of the high calling of God in Christ Jesus" (Philippians 3:13-14).

LIVING INTO THE FUTURE

PHILIPPIANS 3:7–16

Use with Bible Study Guide 11.

WORDS AND PHRASES

Match the words, phrases, or names with the correct definitions.

1. ____ antinomians
2. ____ apprehend
3. ____ faith
4. ____ perfect
5. ____ persistence
6. ____ "reaching forth"
7. ____ righteous
8. ____ rule
9. ____ to "count"
10. ___ works

a. keep on keeping on
b. Christian maturity
c. humanly earned righteousness
d. those without law, living undisciplined lives
e. to consider, esteem, deem or think
f. it is found in the righteousness of Christ
g. a standard
h. to lay hold of, catch or seize; to understand or perceive
i. forgetting past achievements and keeping one's eye on the goal
j. the condition acceptable to God

JUMP-STARTING THE LESSON

11. In terms of "living into the future" what principles can you draw from the In Focus poem?

a. _____

b. _____

c. _____

12. According to the In Focus poem, why mustn't we quit in the fight when we are hardest hit? What can God build in us from the lessons learned in our trials and tribulations—our struggles?

_____.

_____.

_____.

_____.

UNDERSTANDING THE LESSON

13. Why did the apostle Paul begin his letter to the Philippians with some warnings (see Background)?

_____.

_____.

14. According to the apostle Paul, what are four ways that serious Christians can be successful in our walk with Christ—everyday living (Introduction, In Depth)?

a. _____

b. _____

c. _____

d. _____

15. Christ had become both the _____ and _____ for Paul (Philippians 3:8, More Light on the Text).

16. "To know Christ" is not merely to know about Him, but includes a very personal intimacy that interacts with everything Christ did on Earth, which includes (Philippians 3:10, More Light on the Text):

a. _____

b. _____

c. _____

d. _____

17. What are three common mistakes that the apostle Paul addressed that believers make, which can hinder our reaching forth to the goal God has set before us (Philippians 3:13–14, In Depth, More Light on the Text)?

a. _____

b. _____

c. _____

18. Christian maturity entails not only being a hearer of the _____, but a _____ and being _____ into the _____ of Christ (Philippians 3:15, More Light on the Text).

COMMITTING TO THE WORD

19. What are some principles that you have used to help you mature in Christ?

_____

_____

_____

_____

WALKING IN THE WORD

20. Have you already obtained perfection (maturity) in the Lord? Why? Why not?

_____

_____

_____

_____

"Those things, which ye have both learned, and received, and heard, and seen in me, do: and the God of peace shall be with you" (Philippians 4:9).

GROWING IN JOY AND PEACE

PHILIPPIANS 4:2–14

Use with Bible Study Guide 12.

WORDS AND PHRASES

Match the words or names with the correct definitions.

1. _____ "at variance"
2. _____ "be careful for nothing"
3. _____ Clement
4. _____ communicate
5. _____ Euodius
6. _____ moderation
7. _____ "rejoice in the Lord"
8. _____ "shall keep"
9. _____ supplication
10. ___ yokefellow

a. to be aware, attentive, and active in our expression of joy
b. an entreaty or appeal for favor or mercy
c. colleague, comrade, teammate, or spouse
d. God gives His own peace to guard and protect our hearts.
e. having a "falling out"
f. a co-laborer with Paul, who had the role of peacemaker
g. do not worry about anything, don't be anxious
h. to share with, to have fellowship with
i. one of the women in the rift that Paul addressed
j. equity, fairness, gentleness, mildness, or suitability

JUMP-STARTING THE LESSON

11. According to the In Focus excerpt of a poem, "To _____ know _____ is the source of joy."

12. According to the In Focus excerpt, what is the source of a joy-filled life?

_____.

UNDERSTANDING THE LESSON

13. According to the Background section, what three activities did Paul believe that believers should engage in based upon what the Lord has done, is doing, and will do?

a. _____
b. _____
c. _____

14. What does the phrase "rejoice in the Lord" mean (see the Introduction, In Depth)?

a. _____

_____

b. _____

_____

15. What are three reasons that we praise the Lord (Philippians 4:4–7, In Depth)? We praise God for:

a. _____

b. _____

c. _____

16. List two ways that we can rejoice in the Lord (Philippians 4:4–7, In Depth).

a. _____

b. _____

17. God's _____ cures anxiety (Philippians 4:9, In Depth, More Light on the Text).

18. The apostle Paul's contentment was _____ _____ (Philippians 4:11–12, More Light on the Text).

COMMITTING TO THE WORD

19. How have you chosen to rejoice in the Lord, even when you did not feel like rejoicing?

_____

_____

_____

_____

WALKING IN THE WORD

20. Like the apostle Paul, are you content with whatever God chooses to bless you with, whether little or much? Why? Why not?

_____

_____

_____

_____

_____

_____

_____

_____

_____

_____

_____

_____

_____

"And Paul dwelt two whole years in his own hired house, and received all that came in unto him, Preaching the kingdom of God, and teaching those things which concern the Lord Jesus Christ, with all confidence, no man forbidding him" (Acts 28:30–31).

UPHELD BY GOD

ACTS 28:16–25A, 28–31

Use with Bible Study Guide 13.

WORDS AND PHRASES

Match the words or names with the correct definitions.

1. _____ a sect
2. _____ centurion
3. _____ expounded
4. _____ "hired house"
5. _____ Luke
6. _____ salvation
7. _____ Saul of Tarsus
8. _____ testified
9. _____ the kingdom
10. ___ "to be grafted in"

a. the apostle Paul
b. dominion, rule
c. a group following its own tenets or dissensions
d. gave witness to, confirmed a thing by testimony
e. to take the place of the faithless Jews
f. a military officer commanding from 50 to 100 men
g. set forth the way of God, declared
h. rented building
i. the writer of the book of Acts
j. rescue, safety

JUMP-STARTING THE LESSON

11. Do you think that Reverend Jordan handled Ruth's dilemma with wisdom (see the In Focus story)? Why? Why not? _____

_____

_____

12. According to the In Focus story, even though the apostle Paul was in _____ he kept his _____ to share the _____.

UNDERSTANDING THE LESSON

13. The book of Acts gives an account of the _____ and _____ of the Christian church (see Background).

14. How had God showered His favor on the apostle Paul (Acts 28:16, More Light on the Text)?

a. _____

b. _____

c. _____

15. The Roman government tried Paul and wanted to release him, but the Jewish leaders protested (Acts 28:18-20, In Depth, More Light on the Text).　　　True　　　　　False

16. What kind of messiah were the Jews looking for (Acts 28:18-20, More Light on the Text)?

_____

_____

_____

17. From what five books of Moses did the apostle Paul teach the people gathered at his house about the rei̇ or rule of God and about Jesus (Acts 28:23, In Depth, More Light on the Text)?

a. _____　　　b. _____　　　c. _____

d. _____　　　e. _____

18. Both Jews and Gentiles are saved according to their _____ and not because of their

_____ or _____ (Acts 28:28, More Light on the Text).

COMMITTING TO THE WORD

19. Are you committed to the cause of Christ? Why? Why not?

_____

_____

_____

WALKING IN THE WORD

20. How can you use negative circumstances in your life to bring glory to God?

_____

_____

_____

_____

_____

_____

_____

_____

_____

_____

_____

ANSWER KEY

SEPTEMBER–NOVEMBER 2009

Answer Key to Lesson 1

1. j
2. d
3. g
4. h
5. a
6. i
7. e
8. c
9. f
10. b
11. False
12. God, tells
13. Sarah, Lot, Ur, Chaldees
14. Hosea, salvation
15. 40, disobedient, complaining, wilderness
16. "God saves"
17. Deuteronomy
18. wilderness, south, Lebanon, Iraq, Mediterranean
19. Answers will vary.
20. Answers will vary.

Answer Key to Lesson 2

1. e
2. f
3. h
4. j
5. i
6. b
7. c
8. a
9. g
10. d
11. God cuts away a person's self-confidence to compel him or her to admit total inadequacy to do or to be what God desires.
12. God
13. c
14. False
15. sin, disobedience, deliverance, sin

16. Answers will vary.
17. Gideon was hiding the wheat from the Midianites, who would steal it.
18. True
19. perfected, weakness
20. Answers will vary.

Answer Key to Lesson 3
1. c
2. e
3. f
4. g
5. i
6. d
7. j
8. a
9. h
10. b
11. faithfulness, God, careless, His Word
12. d
13. (a) the return of the Jews from their exile in Babylon; (b) the rebuilding of the temple; (c) the launching of social and religious reforms
14. (a) Eleazar, (b) Phineas, (c) Zadok, and (d) Aaron
15. (a) to seek the Law of the LORD, (b) to do it, and (c) to teach God's statutes and ordinances
16. (a) Canaanites, (b) Hittites, (c) Perizzites, (d) Jebusites, (e) Ammonites, (f) Moabites, (g) Egyptians, (h) Amorites
17. True
18. grace, mercy
19. Answers will vary.
20. Answers will vary.

Answer Key to Lesson 4
1. e
2. d
3. f
4. i
5. a
6. g
7. h
8. j
9. b
10. c
11. God
12. total reliance, God
13. love, dedication, faithfulness, God, country
14. faithfulness, authority, problems, wills, desires
15. He cried.
16. True
17. He wanted to keep his mission a secret until he ascertained the magnitude of the damage and extent of the

work to be done, and to hide this from their enemies.

18. False

19. I, hand, God, good, king's words, Let us rise up, build, strengthened, hands, good work

20. Answers will vary.

Answer Key to Lesson 5

1. f
2. h
3. a
4. b
5. g
6. j
7. i
8. c
9. d
10. e
11. life, healing
12. True
13. Jesus Christ, Living God
14. diseases, demons, death
15. He healed her.
16. It helped Him to: (a) keep His faith in His Father strong; (b) follow His Father's will; and (c) overcome Satan.
17. The Levitical law demanded that they be quarantined from the rest of society.
18. born again spiritually
19. Jesus, compassion, his hand, touched, I will, clean
20. Answers will vary.

Answer Key to Lesson 6

1. e
2. h
3. g
4. f
5. a
6. i
7. b
8. j
9. c
10. d
11. Bryant's temper was out of control, and he was not saved.
12. He had been living in the tombs.
13. They were afraid because of the unclean spirits possessing him.
14. He ran and worshiped Him.
15. False
16. True
17. all, issues, problems
18. "The Son of the most high God"
19. We should also worship God.
20. Answers will vary.

Answer Key to Lesson 7

1. g
2. j
3. i
4. f
5. b
6. d
7. h
8. c
9. a
10. e
11. turn, Jesus
12. compassionately, Gentile, physical health
13. compassion, responsiveness, boundaries, race, gender, geography
14. mercy
15. It refers to the priority of the Jews in the preaching of the kingdom of God.
16. (a) fasting, (b) prayer, (c) faith, (d) tenacity (persistence)
17. compassion, love
18. blessings, faith
19. (a) "And she answered and said unto him, Yes, Lord: yet the dogs under the table eat of the children's crumbs." (b) Answers will vary.
20. Answers will vary.

Answer Key to Lesson 8

1. i
2. e
3. d
4. f
5. h
6. a
7. c
8. j
9. g
10. b
11. forsake, follow
12. an actual needle
13. God's grace
14. goodness
15. knew, understood, law, God, Ten Commandments
16. superficial, obedience
17. clearly, eternal life
18. He went away sad because material riches were more important to him than the wealth of eternal life.
19. (a) Jesus, men, impossible, God, God, all, possible; (b) Answers will vary.
20. Answers will vary.

Answer Key to Lesson 9

1. j
2. g
3. d
4. h
5. a
6. c
7. i
8. b
9. e
10. f
11. True
12. imitate Christ, holiness, positive
13. James, John
14. (a) Pontus, (b) Galatia, (c) Cappadocia, (d) Asia, (e) Bithynia
15. trials, persecutions, belief, Lord Jesus Christ
16. holiness
17. The Holy Spirit indwelling us will help us live a holy life.
18. pure heart, holy lifestyle
19. (a) "But as he which hath called you is holy, so be ye holy in all manner of conversation; Because it is written, Be ye holy; for I am holy"; (b) Answers will vary.
20. Answers will vary.

Answer Key to Lesson 10

1. g
2. j
3. i
4. b
5. f
6. c
7. h
8. a
9. e
10. d
11. creation, Jesus, redeem, church, blood
12. election, elect nation
13. God's Word, lifestyle
14. Answers will vary, but should be explained according to John 3:16.
15. undiluted milk
16. (a) chief stone, stone, stumbling; (b) Answers will vary.
17. church, people, God, chosen generation, royal priesthood, holy nation, people, possession
18. mercy
19. (a) chosen generation, royal priesthood, holy nation, peculiar people, praises, him, out, darkness, light; (b) Answers will vary.
20. Answers will vary.

Answer Key to Lesson 11

1. e
2. h
3. g
4. a
5. i
6. j
7. b
8. c
9. f
10. d
11. False
12. willingly, belief, Christ
13. Suffering, salvation
14. Peter instructed Christians to rejoice in their sufferings because the sharing in Christ's suffering is evidence that we will in fact share the many priceless blessings of divine Sonship.
15. Christ, righteousness
16. death, resurrection
17. preached, suffered, martyred, Christ
18. (a) It strengthens the faith of all who endure; (b) it strips away superficial beliefs; and (c) the believers' joyful attitude, while suffering, serves as an example to others.
19. (a) God, own glory; (b) Answers will vary.
20. Answers will vary.

Answer Key to Lesson 12

1. e
2. f
3. h
4. c
5. i
6. a
7. b
8. d
9. j
10. g
11. False
12. Jesus, disciples, hatred, persecution
13. Pentecost, threatened, arrested, beaten
14. intimate relationship, personal knowledge, God, His Son, Jesus Christ
15. faith, Christ, complete
16. character, conduct
17. abundant, entrance, kingdom
18. the written Word of God
19. (a) "According as his divine power hath given unto us all things that pertain unto life and godliness, through the knowledge of him that hath called us to glory and virtue" (2 Peter 1:3); (b) Answers will vary.
20. Answers will vary.

Answer Key to Lesson 13

1. e
2. f
3. h
4. g
5. i
6. c
7. j
8. b
9. d
10. a
11. return, new heaven, new earth
12. The apostle Peter wrote to: (a) warn Christians about false teachers and (b) exhort them to grow in their faith and in the knowledge of their Lord and Savior, Jesus Christ.
13. taught, lazy, walk, Christ
14. truth, God's Word
15. filth, contaminated, heavens, earth
16. everything, humanity, created, invented, built, consumed
17. wrath, destruction, wicked, enemies
18. It is described as a "thief in the night."
19. (a) "The Lord is not slack concerning his promise, as some men count slackness; but is longsuffering to usward, not willing that any should perish, but that all should come to repentance" (2 Peter 3:9); (b) Answers will vary.
20. Answers will vary.

ANSWER KEY

Answer Key to Lesson 1

1. d
2. h
3. i
4. e
5. b
6. c
7. f
8. j
9. g
10. a
11. commitment
12. committing, Jesus, freed, chains, sin
13. Tamar, Canaanite, forbidden
14. (a) Orpah; (b) Ruth
15. Moabite, Moabites, idolaters, Lot
16. c
17. Obed, Jesse, David
18. (a) Abraham; (b) David
19. (a) Tamar, who was an adulteress, (b) Bathsheba, who was an adulteress, (c) Rahab, who was a prostitu and (d) Ruth, who was an idolatress; grace, Lord, salvation
20. Answers will vary.

Answer Key to Lesson 2

1. b
2. i
3. j
4. a
5. h
6. g
7. d
8. f
9. c
10. e
11. His Word
12. Bible, life experiences
13. True
14. brilliant white light

15. Psalm 8:4-6 describes humans as being a little lower than angels.
16. faith, sign, truth, word
17. The virgin birth is very important, because if Jesus had been born to ordinary human beings, He would have inherited the human sin nature and He could not have taken the punishment for our sins. Only a pure, sinless person could die for us.
18. The angel meant that Jesus will occupy an exalted place of honor and rule. He will be called "the son of the highest."
19. Lord, sign, virgin, conceive, son, Immanuel
20. Answers will vary.

Answer Key to Lesson 3

1. e
2. f
3. b
4. i
5. c
6. a
7. j
8. d
9. h
10. g
11. Heavenly Father, Son
12. love, nurture, mentor, leave, forsake
13. "Jewish Gospel," Jewish
14. Holy Spirit
15. (a) virgin birth, Jesus; (b) Answers will vary.
16. God, God
17. True
18. fulfillment, divine purpose
19. bring forth, son, JESUS, save his people, sins
20. Answers will vary.

Answer Key to Lesson 4

1. c
2. g
3. d
4. h
5. b
6. i
7. a
8. j
9. f
10. e
11. Kathy saw that the people of Egypt were brown and black-skinned people like she was and not white-skinned people as portrayed in much Bible art.
12. King Jesus
13. wise men, east, newborn king
14. (a) Herod—outright opposition; (b) Bible scholars—could tell where the Messiah was predicted to be

born, but did not act upon this information; and (c) the wise men—were foreigners, with not much biblical understanding—and yet these were the ones who set aside everything else in their lives to truly know Jesus
15. b
16. Herod had all the baby boys two years old and under in Bethlehem and the surrounding area killed.
17. The reappearance of the star: (a) confirmed the correctness of looking for the child in Bethlehem and (b) guided the wise men to the specific location.
18. Matthew 2:18 speaks of the slaughter of the children and the displacement of Jesus and His family because of Herod's decree.
19. star, rejoiced, exceeding, great, joy
20. Answers will vary.

Answer Key to Lesson 5
1. e
2. g
3. a
4. i
5. j
6. b
7. d
8. c
9. f
10. h
11. Answers will vary.
12. humility, obedience, baptism, humility, Jesus
13. prophet, John, prophet
14. sin, repent, repentance, Jesus, hearts
15. (a) The two men say similar things; (b) they are introduced in a similar fashion; (c) both are opposed by the Pharisees and Sadducees; (d) both appeal to the same generation to repent; (e) both act by the authority of heaven; (f) both are understood by the people to be prophets; (g) both are rejected and executed as criminals; and (h) both are buried by their own disciples.
16. John the Baptist foretold: (a) the coming of Christ and (b) Jesus' baptism of the Holy Spirit.
17. True
18. Father, Son, Holy Spirit
19. (a) heaven, This is my beloved Son, well pleased; (b) Answers will vary.
20. Answers will vary.

Answer Key to Lesson 6
1. e
2. h
3. f
4. j
5. g
6. d
7. a
8. b
9. c
10. i
11. Answers will vary.

12. angel, light, roaring lion
13. Spirit, desert, 40, 40
14. True
15. False
16. Fasting: (a) can be done to help us determine God's will and direction in our life or ministry; (b) to express sorrow for sin; and (c) when we are seeking God's protection.
17. gluttony, glory, greed
18. He used the Word of God (Scripture).
19. Get, thee, hence, Satan, written, worship, Lord, God, him, only, serve
20. Answers will vary.

Answer Key to Lesson 7
1. e
2. f
3. h
4. g
5. j
6. i
7. b
8. a
9. c
10. d
11. faith
12. trust, Savior, Healer, Provider, Jesus Christ
13. d
14. They were looking for a military leader, who would create a new kingdom to rule the land with justice.
15. suffering servant, suffered, humanity
16. Jews
17. Healing was an important part of Jesus' ministry because healing reveals that Jesus cares about humanity.
18. Three parts of Jesus' ministry were: (a) teaching the disciples; (b) preaching God's truth and kingdom; and (c) revealing miracles by faith.
19. "The blind receive their sight, and the lame walk, the lepers are cleansed, and the deaf hear, the dead are raised up, and the poor have the gospel preached to them." (b) Answers will vary.
20. Answers will vary.

Answer Key to Lesson 8
1. f
2. e
3. d
4. g
5. i
6. b
7. h
8. j
9. c
10. a
11. communicate, God, Jesus
12. (a) giving praise; (b) giving thanks; (c) asking for help; and (d) wondering about life
13. power, authority

14. judgment, Israel
15. in the Word of God
16. God's will
17. a change begins within our hearts
18. (a) love, (b) selflessness, (c) humility
19. (a) delivered, me, Son, Father, Father, Son, Son, reveal him; (b) Answers will vary.
20. Answers will vary.

Answer Key to Lesson 9

1. g
2. f
3. i
4. d
5. j
6. a
7. h
8. c
9. e
10. b
11. True
12. trust God, sovereign
13. Kingdom, God, love, God
14. life, prove, Messiah, King
15. Capernaum, Galilee, Nazareth
16. e
17. False
18. "A prophet is not without honor, save in his own country and in his own house" (Matthew 13:57).
19. (a) unbelief; (b) Answers will vary.
20. Answers will vary.

Answer Key to Lesson 10

1. e
2. d
3. g
4. j
5. b
6. h
7. i
8. a
9. c
10. f
11. desperate mother, point, need
12. True
13. such a great faith
14. unclean
15. She cried out, "Lord, Son of David, have mercy on me!"
16. hearts, calling out, Lord, grace
17. False

18. protect, deliver, evil
19. Jesus, her, woman great, faith, even, wilt, daughter, whole, hour
20. Answers will vary.

Answer Key to Lesson 11

1. e
2. c
3. f
4. j
5. d
6. i
7. a
8. b
9. g
10. h
11. True
12. Jews, Messiah, kingdom
13. rejected, killed, "Suffering Servant"
14. grounded, truth
15. (a) Savior, (b) Provider, (c) Healer, (d) Comforter, (e) Intercessor, (f) Friend, (g) Fortress, (h) Father
16. False
17. True
18. (a) total commitment; (b) denying ourselves; (c) taking up our cross; and (d) following Him.
19. (a) I, give, thee, keys, kingdom, heaven, thou, bind, earth, bound, heaven, thou, loose, earth, loosed, heaven; (b) Answers will vary.
20. Answers will vary.

Answer Key to Lesson 12

1. d
2. i
3. b
4. h
5. c
6. g
7. j
8. a
9. e
10. f
11. God's presence confirmed that Jesus is indeed the Son of God.
12. death, resurrection
13. manifested, Jesus Christ
14. Peter, James, John
15. splendor, majesty
16. law, prophets
17. touch
18. fear, sinful
19. (a) "And was transfigured before them: and his face did shine as the sun, and his raiment was white as the light" (Matthew 17:2); (b) Answers will vary.
20. Answers will vary.

Answer Key to Lesson 13

1. h
2. g
3. e
4. d
5. a
6. b
7. c
8. i
9. j
10. f
11. sacrificial offering
12. extravagantly, love
13. destroy, all costs
14. betrayal, crucifixion, Feast, Passover
15. Last Supper
16. True
17. discernment, evil, good
18. burial
19. (a) "Verily I say unto you, Wheresoever this gospel shall be preached in the whole world, there shall also this, that this woman hath done, be told for a memorial of her" (Matthew 26:13); (b) Answers will vary.
20. Answers will vary.

ANSWER KEY

Answer Key to Lesson 1

1. f
2. g
3. h
4. j
5. i
6. b
7. c
8. d
9. a
10. e
11. They prayed aloud for each neighbor; they visited a neighbor, too.
12. Our neighborhoods are ripe with opportunities to witness for Christ.
13. fifth, Minor, Jeroboam II's
14. repentance
15. Assyrians
16. The four infractions are: (a) evil plots against God; (b) exploitation of the helpless; (c) cruelty in war; and (d) idolatry, prostitution, and witchcraft.
17. The four are: (a) the LORD, (b) God's people, (c) God's assignment to go to Nineveh, and (d) the calling on Jonah's life.
18. True
19. Because sometimes Satan's hold is so pronounced (entrenched), there is a need for both prayer and fasting to break the curses—to break the cycle of sin.
20. Answers will vary.

Answer Key to Lesson 2

1. d
2. f
3. i
4. h
5. g
6. b
7. c
8. e
9. j
10. a
11. just, unjust
12. everybody

13. pity party

14. death

15. (a) True; (b) "True repentance" is turning away from sin and turning to a compassionate and merciful God for forgiveness and salvation; must demonstrate faith in God with repentant actions.

16. Jonah was angry with the LORD for bringing honor to a country that he felt did not deserve such grace and mercy (God saved the Ninevites).

17. demise

18. God's harsh judgment is reserved for those who refuse to hear His message of salvation.

19. fled, Tarshish, gracious, merciful, slow, kindness, evil

20. Answers will vary.

Answer Key to Lesson 3

1. c

2. f

3. e

4. a

5. i

6. h

7. d

8. j

9. g

10. b

11. True

12. family, crisis

13. apostasy, oppression, Judges

14. Judah, Moab

15. He did not want His people to intermarry with non-believers in the one, true God; those who might lead them into spiritual adultery.

16. broken, restored

17. selfish, needs

18. Naomi said, "The LORD grant you that ye may find rest."

19. (a) She would go with Naomi wherever she went; (b) She would live with Naomi wherever she lived; (c) She would allow Naomi's people to be her people; and (d) Naomi's God would be her God.

20. Answers will vary.

Answer Key to Lesson 4

1. e

2. f

3. g

4. b

5. h

6. j

7. a

8. d

9. c

10. i

11. Mrs. Coulibaly: (a) brought in some fried plantain for the children to eat; (b) helped the children to find Burkina Faso on the map; (c) wore a beautiful African dress to class; and (d) showed the children

some West African artwork.

12. eyes, hearts

13. Jesus became fully human (made like us without the sin) so that He could offer Himself as a sacrifice for our sins; we have redemption through His blood and the forgiveness of sin.

14. According to God's Law, the corners of the field were not to be harvested and any grain that was dropped was to be left behind to provide food for the poor.

15. humility, compassion

16. True

17. He had acted kindly toward her because she had acted kindly toward Naomi, her mother-in-law.

18. care, protection

19. Boaz and Ruth's son, Obed, became the grandfather of King David, who was the ancestor of our Lord and Savior, Jesus Christ.

20. Answers will vary.

Answer Key to Lesson 5

1. e
2. i
3. f
4. g
5. j
6. b
7. h
8. d
9. c
10. a
11. pain, joy
12. leave, forsake, sorrow, relief, joy
13. True
14. Jesus came into the world to: (a) establish God's kingdom; (b) redeem humanity by His perfect life; and (c) atone for our sins (pay our sin penalty).
15. trust, Jesus, Him, details
16. joy, theirs, Christ
17. Answers will vary, but part of the answer should be "our requests should not be rooted in selfishness, but those which emerge from a desire to do God's will."
18. False
19. not, see, me, see, me, Father
20. Answers will vary.

Answer Key to Lesson 6

1. h
2. g
3. e
4. j
5. f
6. i
7. b
8. c
9. a

10. d

11. believers, love, others, God, loved

12. empowered, love, love, shed, abroad, hearts, Holy Spirit

13. "the sons of thunder"

14. (a) Jesus and John shared a close personal relationship; (b) John was with Jesus during the raising of Jairus' daughter (Luke 8:51); (c) John was with Jesus on the Mount of Transfiguration (Luke 9:28-29); (d) John was with Jesus in the Garden of Gethsemane (Mark 14:32-33); John was with Jesus at His trial and crucifixion (John 18:15-16; 19:26-27); (e) Jesus chose John to care for His mother in His absence (John 19:26-27); (f) John was among those who witnessed the empty tomb (John 20:1-10); and (g) John was among those who witnessed the Risen Christ (John 20:19-20; 21:1-2).

15. believes, right, right, light, maintain, truth, apostolic teaching, believers, blinded, darkness

16. state, moral, darkness, Christ's deliverance

17. sacrificially, Christ

18. lifestyle, committed

19. serve, two, masters, hate, one, love, other, devoted, despise, God, money

20. Answers will vary.

Answer Key to Lesson 7

1. j

2. h

3. g

4. f

5. c

6. a

7. i

8. e

9. d

10. b

11. thoughts

12. center, thoughts, emotions, director

13. Mosaic Law

14. c

15. (a) You must not have any other god but me; (b) You must not make for yourself an idol; (c) You must not misuse the name of the LORD your God; and (d) Remember to observe the Sabbath day by keeping it holy.

16. (a) "To love your neighbor as yourself" (Leviticus 19:18, NLT); (b) Honor your father and mother; (b) You must not murder; (c) You must not commit adultery; (d) You must not steal; (e) You must not testify falsely against your neighbor; and (f) You must not covet anything that belongs to your neighbor.

17. love, legalism

18. love, God, loving one's neighbor

19. (a) "Jesus said unto him, Thou shalt love the Lord thy God with all thy heart, and with all thy soul, and with all thy mind" (Matthew 22:37); (b) Answers will vary.

20. Answers will vary.

Answer Key to Lesson 8

1. d
2. f
3. j
4. g
5. h
6. e
7. i
8. b
9. a
10. c
11. Kirk needed spiritual revival or restoration ("a banquet for his soul"), too.
12. Those who have accepted Jesus Christ as their Lord and Savior will be a part of God's kingdom.
13. Five attributes of humility are: (a) it allows us to acknowledge that God has a claim on our lives; (b) it allows us to acknowledge that we make mistakes and are mortal creatures; (c) it allows us to acknowledge that God is the Master of the universe; (d) the humble person can say, "I am a sinner, and I need to be saved"; and (e) humility is an ingredient of wisdom.
14. False
15. laws
16. The personal invitation is believe on the Lord Jesus Christ so that we might be saved (John 3:16).
17. faith, Christ Jesus
18. one, only, Son, spiritually, needy
19. (a) "Go out quickly into the streets and lanes of the city, and bring in hither the poor, and the maimed, and the halt, and the blind" (Luke 14:21); (b) Answers will vary.
20. Answers will vary.

Answer Key to Lesson 9

1. e
2. i
3. f
4. g
5. h
6. j
7. d
8. a
9. c
10. b
11. His kingdom
12. It helps us to see that we have the power of God in us and we are able to share the Gospel with others.
13. d
14. Philemon's
15. It told them of the grace of God found in the person of Jesus Christ.
16. (a) Gnosticism; (b) the Gnostics believed and taught that it took special knowledge for anyone to be accepted by God, even Christians.
17. It transformed their lives (brought forth fruit).
18. empowered, endurance, patience, forbearance, joy
19. Answers will vary.
20. Answers will vary.

Answer Key to Lesson 10

1. g
2. i
3. j
4. f
5. a
6. h
7. c
8. d
9. b
10. e
11. It can: (a) cause great confusion in a church body; and (b) draw people away from the rudiments of the Gospel message.
12. Believers need to: (a) be exhorted and reminded of the fullness we have in Christ; and (b) stay rooted in the faith.
13. ministry, death, resurrection
14. instruction, encouragement
15. God's mystery is Christ Himself.
16. Paul told them to: (a) stand firm; (b) stick to what they have been taught (the foundational truths); and (c) continue to have a thankful heart.
17. Jewish, legalism, Gnosticism
18. apostles, faithful
19. Answers will vary.
20. Answers will vary.

Answer Key to Lesson 11

1. g
2. e
3. f
4. a
5. b
6. h
7. i
8. j
9. c
10. d
11. virtues, Jesus, Christ
12. True
13. "Election" specifically refers to a choice God made before creation to have a people for Himself.
14. False
15. We should get rid of "sinful things" within us.
16. (a) mercy, (b) kindness, (c) humbleness, (d) meekness, (e) longsuffering, (f) forbearance, (g) forgiveness, (h) charity (love), and (i) the peace of God
17. The apostle Paul taught that because Christ has forgiven us of our sins and made us "a new man"—"a new creation"—and our sins were heinous beyond imagining and offensive to God's character, others' sins pale in comparison to our own. Therefore, we should be willing to forgive our fellow man.
18. The apostle Paul felt that "the peace of God" should serve as judge over our hearts—it must reign over us.
19. Answers will vary.
20. Answers will vary.

Answer Key to Lesson 12

1. c
2. e
3. f
4. g
5. i
6. h
7. a
8. j
9. b
10. d
11. Answers will vary.
12. jail, Good, News, Onesimus
13. There was ambiguity because Roman law recognized that slaves were human beings, but they were also considered property.
14. F, fugitive
15. house arrest
16. authority, compassion, service, brotherhood
17. (a) forgive Onesimus and (b) accept Onesimus as a brother
18. condemn, condone, transform relationships
19. Answers will vary.
20. Answers will vary.

Answer Key to Lesson 13

1. d
2. h
3. i
4. e
5. a
6. b
7. c
8. j
9. g
10. f
11. Jude warned his readers to: (a) remain faithful to Jesus Christ; and (b) not to live immoral lives.
12. Answers will vary.
13. "Antinomianism" is the belief that since faith alone is necessary for salvation, believers do not need to obey any moral laws. It is spirituality without restrictions, which Jude taught against.
14. True
15. (a) people want to live without rules; and (b) there's a refusal to believe that Jesus was fully God and fully man.
16. The heretics: (a) created factions and split communities; (b) followed animalistic (sensual) instincts; and (c) lacked the Spirit of God.
17. Answers will vary.
18. Answers will vary, but should include: Jude emphasized the purity of the Christian faith; that God is holy (set apart from sin); that Christians have been made holy and that our faith is "the most holy faith." Therefore, the Holy Spirit will help us to pray to a holy God, in His will and not selfishly.
19. Answers will vary.
20. Answers will vary.

ANSWER KEY

JUNE–AUGUST 2010

Answer Key to Lesson 1

1. f
2. e
3. j
4. i
5. h
6. g
7. b
8. c
9. d
10. a
11. Clara was persecuted because she professed faith in Christ and would not join in her family's parties and trips to the casinos to gamble.
12. Clara simply, quietly lived out her faith.
13. They were struggling with their newfound faith.
14. There were misunderstandings concerning Christ's second coming.
15. (a) to encourage these young believers; (b) to assure them of his love; (c) to praise them for their faithfulness in spite of their circumstances; and (d) to remind them of their hope in Christ
16. (a) service, (b) loving deeds, and (c) anticipation of Jesus' return
17. True
18. (a) They had turned away from idols; (b) they had turned to the One True and Living God; (c) they had turned away from their sin; and (d) they looked forward to Jesus' second coming.
19. death, sorrow, crying, pain
20. Answers will vary.

Answer Key to Lesson 2

1. d
2. f
3. h
4. g
5. b
6. i
7. j
8. e
9. c
10. a
11. (a) integrity, (b) accountability
12. commitment, God
13. d

14. serve, Gospel, opposition
15. (a) deceit, (b) uncleanness, (c) guile and flattery, (d) covetousness, (e) glory
16. True
17. False
18. faith
19. Answers will vary.
20. Answers will vary.

Answer Key to Lesson 3
1. f
2. c
3. g
4. e
5. h
6. j
7. i
8. a
9. b
10. d
11. They came together to pray and encourage one another.
12. Paul sent Timothy to encourage the Thessalonians, who were experiencing persecution.
13. d
14. It was cut short due to persecution.
15. His sole purpose was "to establish…and comfort" them in their faith (1 Thessalonians 3:2).
16. steal, kill, destroy
17. (a) Paul requested that God provide a means for him to get back to visit Thessalonica; (b) petitioned God to help the believers' love to grow for one another and others; and (c) requested for God to strengthen the believers at Thessalonica to be blameless and holy before God.
18. The apostle Paul desired that the church might "abound" in love so that the Lord might establish their hearts blamelessly in holiness.
19. Answers will vary.
20. Answers will vary.

Answer Key to Lesson 4
1. e
2. g
3. f
4. i
5. d
6. a
7. j
8. c
9. h
10. b
11. pure, holy, garbage
12. pleasing
13. through, through
14. (a) our position in Christ and (b) our practical walk in our daily lives.
15. (a) Positional sanctification is a work of the Father; (b) Practical sanctification is achieved by believers

separating from all that is unclean and unholy; and (c) by believers recognizing the members of our bodies as holy instruments of God for the accomplishment of His holy purposes.

16. True
17. False
18. True
19. Answers will vary.
20. Answers will vary.

Answer Key to Lesson 5

1. f
2. e
3. i
4. h
5. j
6. a
7. d
8. c
9. b
10. g
11. The policeman told Brandon that, in his experience, "thieves never showed up when people were looking for them, but always when they were least expected."
12. thief, night
13. heavens, shout
14. Jesus, Father
15. (a) awake, (b) sensitive, (c) alert, and (d) prepared
16. The Thessalonians became a part through faith in the Gospel of Christ.
17. True
18. faith, love
19. Answers will vary.
20. Answers will vary.

Answer Key to Lesson 6

1. e
2. c
3. i
4. g
5. j
6. h
7. a
8. b
9. d
10. f
11. Answers will vary, but should entail the fact that our strength comes for the Lord, who made heaven and Earth; and sometimes while experiencing the hardships of life, our strength can fail us if we don't lean and depend on Almighty God.
12. False
13. Paul, Silas, Timothy
14. Answers will vary.
15. The intercessors prayed that: (a) God would make the believers at Thessalonica worthy of the life to

which He called them to, and (b) that He would also empower them to live for Him.

16. Answers will vary, but should include: It is through faith that we receive Christ's righteousness in place of our own unrighteousness.

17. faith, love

18. Answers will vary, but it might include: God is so holy and powerful, beyond our comprehension, that the purifying and destructive force of fire is an appropriate way for us to understand that mighty holiness.

19. The absence of God's sustaining presence is an element of the misery of hell.

20. Answers will vary.

Answer Key to Lesson 7

1. f
2. d
3. e
4. g
5. a
6. b
7. i
8. j
9. c
10. h

11. They knew that the Lord had them still in their present church's vineyard because there were many who were spiritually sick and needed to be taught God's Word.

12. His, lost souls, build His kingdom

13. faith, trust, God

14. Both (a) build up the church and (b) build character in the believer who fights the good fight of faith.

15. True

16. Answers will vary, but should include: false doctrines lead to confusion among believers; may cause believers to fall into sins such as idleness and meddling.

17. commit, foundational truths

18. God, through His Holy Spirit, will help believers to walk (live) in His will and ways. Only He can establish us in His ways.

19. God showed His unconditional love by sending His one and only Son, Jesus Christ, so that sinners could believe in Him and be saved.

20. Answers will vary.

Answer Key to Lesson 8

1. i
2. f
3. g
4. h
5. j
6. c
7. d
8. a
9. e
10. b

11. Robert realized that he had given up on his commitment to help save the lives of the people in the neighborhood where the clinic was by educating them about HIV/AIDS and substance abuse. He had become "weary in well doing."

12. Answers will vary.

13. Prayer

14. It is imperative because Satan is constantly waging war against the spread of the Gospel.

15. Answers will vary.

16. Answers will vary.

17. Holy, Spirit, love, God

18. The time of withdrawal was to make the perpetrators ashamed of their actions—their disobedience. Then they would come back into fellowship as obedient servants of God.

19. Answers will vary.

20. Answers will vary.

Answer Key to Lesson 9

1. h
2. i
3. f
4. e
5. g
6. a
7. b
8. j
9. d
10. c

11. To live means that "we exhibit enthusiasm and excitement in all that we do, that we face challenges boldly and confidently because life has much to offer."

12. Jesus Christ, righteousness

13. prison

14. joy, gratitude

15. He was rejoicing because Christ was preached.

16. For Paul, "death" is gaining the unmediated presence of Christ and "life" can offer more service to God.

17. To live as a "citizen of heaven" means: (a) our conduct should be appropriate for citizens of God's kingdom; (b) believers need to stand together; (c) believers should not be fighting one another; and (d) believers need to present a united front against our real enemy—Satan and his kingdom.

18. privilege

19. Answers will vary.

20. Answers will vary.

Answer Key to Lesson 10

1. f
2. h
3. g
4. c
5. i
6. a
7. b
8. d
9. j
10. e
11. ourselves

12. humanity, died, Cross

13. The Kenosis speaks of Christ's: (a) eternal deity, (b) incarnation, (c) humiliation, (d) death, (e) resurrection, and (f) exaltation via ascension.

14. False

15. (a) Paul appealed to the church members' spiritual and personal relationships, and (b) for their unity and humility.

16. Saviour, Jesus Christ

17. mind, love, spirit, purpose

18. Sanctification is: (a) inspired by the Spirit; (b) enabled by the Spirit; and (c) produces the fruit of the Spirit.

19. Answers will vary.

20. Answers will vary.

Answer Key to Lesson 11

1. d

2. h

3. f

4. b

5. a

6. i

7. j

8. g

9. e

10. c

11. Answers will vary.

12. Answers will vary.

13. Paul began with warnings because some false teachers were telling believers that they could not be saved by faith alone, but had to supplement their faith with keeping certain Jewish laws and rituals.

14. Believers can be successful if we: (a) keep focused on the gains in Christ; (b) keep focused on the knowledge of Christ; (c) keep focused on harmony with Christ; and (d) keep moving toward Christian maturity.

15. goal, prize

16. It includes: (a) His humility and approachability; (b) His love and compassion; (c) His suffering and death; and (d) His ultimate victory and resurrection.

17. The common mistakes are dwelling on: (a) past bad decisions, mistakes, selfish or mean acts, etc.; (b) past exceptional Christian service, such as a mission trip or major sacrifices; and (c) prior worldly accomplishments and glories, which can create a false sense of importance and expectations.

18. Word, doer, transformed, image

19. Answers will vary.

20. Answers will vary.

Answer Key to Lesson 12

1. e

2. g

3. f

4. h

5. i

6. j

7. a

9. b

10. c

11. truly, the Lord

12. To love the Lord with all your heart is the source of a joy-filled life.

13. Believers should: (a) stand firm in the Lord (Philippians 4:1); (b) be united in the Lord (vv. 2-3); and (c) rejoice in the Lord (vv. 4-20).

14. It means: (a) to be aware that as Christians, the Lord is the Source of our joy, so we will not spend time, money, thought, or energy seeking joy in the wrong places; and (b) to develop a relationship with the Lord so that we will not cut off, or in any way hinder the flow of the joy that the Lord gives.

15. We praise God for: (a) what He has done; (b) what He is doing; and (c) what He is going to do.

16. We can rejoice in the Lord by: (a) living in moderation and (b) trusting in God.

17. peace

18. God-sufficient

19. Answers will vary.

20. Answers will vary.

Answer Key to Lesson 13

1. c

2. f

3. g

4. h

5. i

6. j

7. a

8. d

9. b

10. e

11. Answers will vary.

12. prison, commitment, Gospel

13. birth, growth

14. God had showered His favor on Paul because Paul could: (a) dwell by himself (in his own house instead of with other prisoners); (b) receive visitors; and (c) still engage in ministry.

15. True

16. They were looking for an earthly, military messiah, a king to come and overthrow the Roman government and set them free from their enemies.

17. The five books of Moses are: (a) Genesis, (b) Exodus, (c) Leviticus, (d) Numbers, and (e) Deuteronomy.

18. faith, culture, heritage

19. Answers will vary.

20. Answers will vary.